JONI MITCHELL

LADY OF THE CANYON

WRITTEN BY

MICHAEL O'NEILL

sona BOOKS

First published in the UK 2020 by Sona Books an imprint of Danann Publishing Ltd.

CAT NO: SON0445

Photography courtesy of

Getty images:

- Jack Robinson/Hulton Archive
- Robert Altman/Michael Ochs Archives
- RB/Redferns
- Central Press/Stringer
- Tony Russell/Redferns
- Rolls Press/Popperfoto
- GAB Archive/Redferns
- 20th Century Fox/Handout
- Gijsbert Hanekroot/Redferns
- Donaldson Collection/Michael Ochs Archives

- Ginny Winn/Michael Ochs Archives
- Mike Slaughter/Toronto Star
- Michael Ochs Archives/Stringer
- Ed Perlstein/Redferns
- Jeff Goode/Toronto Star
- Gary Gershoff
- Roger Ressmeyer/Corbis/VCG
- Richard McCaffrey/Michael Ochs Archive
- Michael Putland
- Pete Still/Redferns

- Ebet Roberts/Redferns
- Calle Hesslefors/ullstein bild
- Doug Griffin/Toronto Star
- David Redfern/Redferns
- Ken Hively/Los Angeles Times
- Frank Micelotta/ImageDirect
- Frederick M. Brown/Stringer
- Vivien Killilea/Stringer
- Stephanie Rayn Barnett

Book layout & design Darren Grice at Ctrl-d
copy editor Juliette O'Neill

Made in EU.
ISBN: 978-1-912918-24-9

CONTENTS

INTRODUCTION 8

WIND IN MY HAIR 10

THE AGONY AND THE ECSTASY 14

GOLDEN YEARS 32

CHANGING HER TUNE 50

THE DRUNK WITH SAGE'S EYES 72

ROADS LESS TRAVELLED 80

FROM LOVE TO VIOLENCE AND BACK AGAIN 96

SIZZLE AND FRY MUSIC 106

A MEETING WITH THE PAST 114

THE CIRCLE CLOSES 126

DISCOGRAPHY 130

INTRODUCTION

From a remote north-western community in Canada to folk and pop icon, Joni Mitchell, the quintessential singer songwriter, went on to move fearlessly between musical genres, to explore the depths of the human journey in songs that ruthlessly dissected her own jagged edges and those of her generation and lay them out for public consideration.

Joni Mitchell's image is burned into the history of 1960 and 1970s popular music in the unmatched way that is granted to very few others. She strides atop the pantheon that contains such rarified names as Leonard Cohen and Bob Dylan or Tom Waits. Her influence has reached out through the ensuing decades permeating through to female artists from Madonna to Taylor Swift.

Her real-life pain marbled her music; recovering from polio at the age of nine and giving her daughter up for adoption after she became pregnant in 1964, were seminal moments in a career of superlatives.

When she felt that she needed to expand her musical horizons, she moved away from the early albums such as Ladies of the Canyon and Blue that had caused her to be oppressed by, and to squirm away from, the tentacles of fame, towards luscious, glossy pop on Court and Spark and then on into her private musical realms of rhythmically complex, jazz-oriented albums, working with greats such as Herbie Hancock and Charlie Mingus.

When she was on top of the wave, Joni Mitchell, employing innovative harmonics, her voice swooping upwards in the middle of a word, and changing her guitar tuning almost after each song, was one of the most courageous, caustically honest and talented artists of the her era, adventurous, and a magnetic pole of inspiration to many of the women who followed her into the shark-infested waters of the music industry, an artist who defied conventional borders between gender or musical genres. Rejecting labels, she insisted that she was not a feminist, and as a sharp critic of the music industry, she always insisted on artistic control of her work, retaining the publishing rights for her music.

As Rolling Stone mused, "Not bad for a girl who had no voice training, hated to read in school, and learned guitar from a Pete Seeger instruction record."

WIND IN MY HAIR

Myrtle Marguerite (McKee) and William Andrew Anderson's daughter Roberta Joan Anderson, saw the light of day in Fort Macleod, Alberta, Canada, on the 7th of November 1943. Myrtle was a teacher who boasted Scottish and Irish ancestry, whilst William had Norwegian roots and worked for the Royal Canadian Air Force as a flight lieutenant.

Joni was self-aware even at a young age, aware enough to sense that her parents were not, perhaps, the able parents they should have been, which led to her feeling that she was vulnerable to the vagaries of their behaviour and that her father needed protecting. Myrtle and William were undemonstrative, though friendly people, and yet within his quiet exterior, William harboured a sharp competitive spirit, which seems to have been the midwife to Joni's less introverted, combative nature. But the young girl also felt that her parents were strapped to their social and mental tramlines and unable to contemplate a wider vision of the world – one which she would later explore in complex detail.

After the Second World War had ended, when her father decided to run a grocery store, the family settled into a decent, middle-class existence. School life was problematic once Joni had decided that if all you had to do to get praise was to learn by heart then school wasn't for her. From that early age on, she rejected any attempt to slot her into the system. And this wrenching torsion between the low waterline that could be accepted as success in the world, and her need to be acknowledged by that world for what she was, caused friction in Joni for her entire musical career. But "sell out", as she described it, she never could, whatever raw nerves that attitude might touch and set jangling.

Until the age of five, Joni had one companion she could rely on, at least; her name was Sharon Bell, whose name, evoking memories, would resurface many years later in Song for Sharon. And then there was music. Although she played no instrument at that age, she would visit music competitions to listen and deconstruct the music she heard, – once a year to North Battleford to hear Sharon compete. Possessed of a sharp critical sense even then, she would listen keenly to the adjudicators criticisms, often finding fault with their judgements, but learning by listening.

Music was always an escape from the life that she found suspect, and from the angst-filled teenagers around her in school discussing the world's problems; Elvis and Chuck Berry, dancing and painting helped her distance herself from what she perceived to be the psuedo-intellectualism of other school students. And also from the grip of the church and its Bible filled with contradictions.

She revelled in being "Good-time Charley", and yet beneath that brittle, extroverted exterior hiding the hurt of rejection, of belittlement, she found that the wounding shards that her lovers, friends and her industry would throw at her were hard to cope with. Little wonder then, that she began to build the structures for her own separate world within the larger world, in which she could live alone.

The world outside was not devoid of pleasures, however, many of which the Canadian countryside delivered endlessly; the freedom to roam without shoes beneath the open skies of the prairies and listen to the birds singing. She loved the countryside, and these were pleasures that Joni's mind would recall in later years when the pressures of being Joni Mitchell became too great. Nonetheless, the countryside of her early years could not nourish her creative passions; she needed to find whatever was hovering beyond the horizon.

In 1953, a polio epidemic struck Canada. Amongst those it struck down were Neil Young and Joni Mitchell. Joni had been complaining of feeling tired, until one day she couldn't get out of her bed. When she was diagnosed, she was sent to St Paul's Hospital in Saskatoon, where the terrifying wheezing of iron lungs intensified the fear of permanent paralysis and even death. She lost the use of the muscles of her inner legs and back, and the disease caused her spine to be crooked and arch. She feared that, at the very least, she would never walk again.

Her hospitalisation and isolation were made more intolerable by hospital rules – parents were allowed only one half-hour visit on a Sunday – and the instruction to remain motionless, because if she moved, the polio would spread. In fact, Joni remembers that her father never came to visit her in hospital and her mother only came to see her once to bring her a Christmas tree.

But Joni refused to accept her apparent fate; she determined not to become a victim and focused all her energy on the battle for health, on making the basic therapies effective, until the day came, one year later, when she "amazed them by standing up and walking".

She celebrated her return to humanity by dancing, possessed now of an inner strength and self-reliance that would withstand the onslaughts to come. Her experience of hospital had fused all the separate strands of her creative life, her voice, her body, her willpower, into the raw material for the woman she would become. Finally allowed to go home, she joined a choir, singing the descant

12

parts – and was introduced to cigarettes for the first time; she would smoke for the rest of her life.

It was also from around that time, when she was told by a church minister that the story of Adam and Eve was simply symbolic, a revelation to her, that Joni's interest in that fabled garden turned into a lifelong quest to retrieve it, and warn of the damage done to it since.

When she was eleven and the family was living in Saskatoon, one teacher opened the door to a secret garden for her in which she would live from then on; the garden of words. A rebel in his own right, Arthur Kratzmann became her hero, a man who recognised her creative talent, who taught her to kill her clichés, the value of compassionate discernment, and not to measure herself against others; to him she would later dedicate a song on her first album, Song to a Seagull. It was Kratzmann who changed the points for Joni to follow in her musical life when he told her that if she could paint with a brush she could paint with words and that she had to "learn to paint and write in your own blood". As she grew older, Joni would always find an affinity with those like Kratzmann, or Picasso, who danced on the periphery.

Her sense of being devoid of talent fed into her questioning other school systems that denied freethinking and seemed designed only to produce students from a mould. In her own mind during this time, she considered herself to be a painter; writing and music had not yet forced their way to the surface.

As she entered adolescence, the conflict with her "exceedingly proper" mother continued, with Myrtle hurtling accusations that Joni was a liar and a lesbian and, after Joni had shoplifted a pair of pants, a thief. Joni responded by distancing herself even more from her mother's conservative worldview. She became friends with Native Americans, revelling in being just one of the boys, and acquiring a reputation for being provocative. The dichotomy between her world and the 'other' world became clearer as her school report indicated; "Joan does not relate well". Nonetheless, Myrtle took pride in her daughter whenever she could and instilled in Joni a sense of her being special that never left her.

As none of her friends could play a musical instrument, Joni, bought a ukulele so that she and her mates could sit down by the river singing dirty songs and drinking beer. The instrument came in handy for parties, too, and she bought it just at the time when folk music was rising back to the surface. She practised with vice-like determination against the spitting sarcasm of her mother and the pleading of her friends. After all, she had saved the money for it herself after her mother had refused to buy her a guitar. There was no way she was going to give it up.

The young girl was at the forefront of a new sensitivity redefining womanhood in the 1950s; Joni had clearly begun to define her own life and search for her role in the world, and her self-made clothes were just the outward symbols indicating the chameleon within. She knew what was hip – at 16 she was writing a column in the school newspaper called "Fads and fashion" – and she knew already that hip was a "herd mentality", it came and went at somebody's whim and was not a thing to hang your hat on.

Gradually, Joni was disentangling herself from her young life, from the years she had spent yearning for a way to live that lay beyond the life she had hitherto known.

THE AGONY & THE ECSTASY

Having reached the end of her high school career after re-sitting physics, chemistry and maths exams, the only way forward that Joni could see led through art school, which she financed through fashion modelling. Yet even at the Alberta College of Art and Design in Calgary, she found herself splashing around in a sea of minimalism and commercialism when she craved to explore the messy depths of human emotions, love especially, and relationships. She held on for a year before abandoning her studies, although not her love of painting.

It was around this time that she finally bought a guitar and a Pete Seeger instruction record. But her left-hand, weakened by polio, hampered her. Quickly bored with following the rules, she invented her own and applied them to her guitar playing and her singing. She practised singing in a low voice until her octaves helped fuse her sound into a unique style, and then, armed with a selection of folk songs, took the entire package along to audition for John Uren's Depression Club in Calgary. It was there, on September the 13th 1964, that she started out on her musical career playing three sets a night. She displayed the same confidence, the same complicated hide-and-seek personality that would affect everyone she met.

She also became pregnant.

She'd met tall and amiable Brad McMath in art school at a time when she was ready to lose her virginity. They were not a couple; "It was my own stupid fault" she mused later.

They left Calgary for Toronto, and then Brad left her for California.

She had fallen for the cliché, and another dramatic and painful experience that she would try to exorcise in her songs. And when she realised that she had the ability to do just that, she understood that whatever happened, she was master of her own liberation.

Alone now and pregnant, she would need all her musical skills to stay alive. She sang to eat and scrape a living at the best of the worst clubs, unable to afford the fees for the musician's union. She attracted help; people remembered her as being not only beautiful but kind and vulnerable, as though her trials and tribulations had blunted her sharp edges.

On the 19th of February 1965, she gave birth to a daughter, Kelly Dale Anderson. Unsure what to do, without the money for the rent, she gave Kelly into the care of foster parents, certain only, that going back to her parents was not an option. At that moment, the world seemed a terrifying place and her path obscured and equally terrifying. Kelly looked like her mother.

At this low point, she met the tall and handsome American Chuck Mitchell, already an established folksinger and older than she. There was a hope in her mind that after she had moved in with him in Detroit, they would perform as a duo and then rescue Kelly when they had enough money. Love there was, but not enough to stretch it out over a lifetime. Chuck would drop sarcastic comments about her country girl, kitsch roots, and the barbs struck home dragging her resentment into the years that followed.

Joni, a cigarette permanently dangling from her lips, cheered up the dull apartment in Detroit with second-hand furniture and materials in green hues. They made a little money, but Kelly's fate hung like an ominous cloud over their lives. Finally, the decision was made and the adoption papers bearing Joni's signature were handed over. Now there was nothing between Joni and her music.

Back in Detroit, her career began to stabilise. The songs rolled from her pen. She gigged the biggest club in town, the Chessmate, and could now count many prominent folk singers as friends. They both thrived in an atmosphere that provided hope for the future; and Chuck was ambitious. He helped Joni start a publishing company. She was still writing songs, and whilst she enjoyed the domestication of married life, she was very much aware of the little voice within calling her to roam over the next hill. His "cornball", as Joni described it, choice of music also sowed its own discontent in a woman looking forwards and not to the past. Here was a singer who was probing her own talent with open chords and dropped tunings – introduced to them by fellow musician Eric Andersen, but adapting them to produce sounds the like of which no one had ever heard before. Anderson had shown her an open G tuning, which, being a banjo tuning, had been used by blues players - and also by Keith Richards. From then on, she never wanted to sound like anyone else, confounding even players of the calibre of Eric Clapton in her relentless search for sounds that would excite her, sounds that were fresh, and often alighting on the sus chords, chords of suspension as Wayne Shorter called them, that would make a phrase sound unresolved. Joni enjoyed moving from sus chord to sus chord to build tension, in her search for unusual chordal colours and combinations. Her unique style of play would often cause conflicts with musicians trained in the conventional way of playing music, as her style broke all the traditional rules they had been taught. It was a long road and there were many tussles to endure trying to find musicians who were prepared to go with her flow.

Joni and Chuck had married in June 1965. Joni wore a dress she had made herself, and she took the name of Mitchell.

By the autumn of 1965, she was well known enough to appear

RIGHT:

Contact sheet of Joni Mitchell, 1968

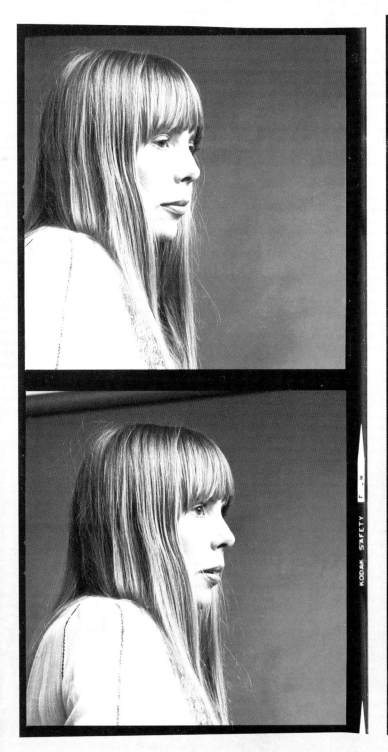

ABOVE:

Contact sheet of Joni Mitchell, 1968

on the 'Let's Sing Out' folk music program on TV. Joni Anderson became Joni Mitchell, and as far as she was concerned, Joni Mitchell was no longer a folksinger, her songs were not folksongs. The climb to widespread recognition had begun – as had the crumbling of the marriage.

Joni would appear several times on the 'Let's Sing Out' show over the next two years, but she and Mitch began to perform separately; she was well aware that she was the attraction, that people came to hear her songs and listen to her unusual musical harmonies and stories of fragile defiance. As James Taylor put it, Joni trained herself; she builds the canvas and applies the paint, she invents the chords. And he might have added, she exudes the words. She felt that Chuck was holding her back, and she was not alone in that opinion. The marriage was stifling her, and once she felt her freedom onstage she wanted it back in her life offstage. The marriage was finally dissolved in 1967. Joni was 23.

She left Detroit and moved to New York, where she enhanced her reputation by playing in clubs up and down the East Coast, booking herself into clubs in North Carolina, South Carolina or Philadelphia besides playing coffeehouses in New York. It was hard work.

It was 1968, and she met the man who would become her first manager, Elliot Roberts from the William Morris talent agency, who would prove invaluable to her career. At last, she had found someone who was proud of her, someone who would defend her.

Buffy Sainte-Marie had recommended that Elliot go to see Joni, a marvellous singer she had said, and when Elliot did so, he remembered being overwhelmed by the incredible songs from someone he had never heard of. As he followed her around the folk clubs as her manager, paying for himself out of his own pocket, he began to formulate a plan for how he would guide her career. Taking a leaf from Bob Dylan's book, he decided that chart hits or extensive radio airtime were not going to work.

Instead, they would play the long game, gradually infiltrating listeners' lives so that her music would become the soundtrack to their everyday existence.

It proved difficult to get a record deal for this beautifully gifted and hard-working woman. The folk revival had withered on the stalk giving way to rock 'n' roll, so Joni was swimming against the tide, and even though the executives thought that their wives would enjoy the music, no one wanted to sign her. What did wives know, after all.

Joni had been convinced that it would not be long before she would be unemployed again, as folk music was on its last legs, and she was not prepared to share her meagre gains with Elliot or anyone else. Nonetheless, they toured together for a month and then she agreed that they could work together. One lesson that she took from those early days was that "the bulk of the people, the mass of the people, really, cannot formulate their own opinion". From that point on, she would try to formulate it for them.

1967 was the same year that she wrote what was, perhaps, the most iconic song of her career, inspired by the Saul Bellow novel Henderson the Rain King; it was called Both Sides, Now and was a classic excavation of a theme through several reprises, a method of song construction that Joni would often use. Chuck had dismissed the song when he heard it.

Al Kooper, on the other hand, musician and producer and a master at spotting and utilising a fleeting opportunity, knew that he had heard a winning song when Joni played it to him at 3 o'clock in the morning in her apartment at 41 W. 16th Street. And he knew what to do next. He grabbed the phone. Judy Collins answered. Joni played again. She knew, of course, that for a songwriter on the way upwards, but surviving from one gig to another, despite her songs being performed by the likes of Buffy Sainte-Marie, Judy Collins could swing doors open wide. Judy Collins was making an album, and she was thunderstruck when

she heard the song. Of course she wanted to sing it, sing its words of gentle wonderment at illusion and disillusion.

And yet, the whirling pools of Joni's character would never allow her to 'forgive' Judy for whatever harm she felt had been done to her song – perhaps it was too saccharine a rendition for its more abrasive author – despite the fact that the recording was the initial propulsion beneath Joni's rise to stardom. She would, grudgingly, accept that if there had been a turning point in her life it came with the recording of her songs by Tom Rush and Judy Collins, and that as the songwriter, she was then able to play in some of the clubs that Tom Rush played in. She also confessed, referring to Both Sides, Now, that she "would have liked to have sung it myself", primarily because she would have liked to have been the one to "have swung it".

And not only that.

Judy Collins was responsible for another brief but passionate period in Joni's life, one which would affect her musical life deeply, when Judy persuaded the organisers of the Newport Festival to allow Joni and another young singer to perform there. The singer's name was Leonard Cohen.

At the time, Cohen was known as a poet and novelist rather than a musician, and at 33 years of age, he was nine years older than Joni Mitchell. His musicianship was hardly likely to impress the young girl, but as a wordsmith she fell under his spell. She heard him sing Suzanne, and in common with the rest of the world, she loved it. Suddenly, she felt that all her songs were naive in comparison, and coming up against Cohen not only made her feel humble, it made her realise she had to raise the standard of her songwriting.

Like Collins, Cohen, too, would later feel the sting of her caustic sarcasm when she dismissed him as a "boudoir poet", disappointed that he had used others' words, gasping, almost, for originality, although she did so increasingly herself. She

ABOVE:
Portrait of Joni Mitchell, 1968

MAIN IMAGE:

**Musician Joni Mitchell recording her first
album "Song to a Seagull" at Sunset Sound
Recorders in 1967 in Los Angeles, California**

Posed portrait of Joni Mitchell

LEFT:

Posed portrait of Joni Mitchell

made the distinction between stealing from life and stealing from books; the former acceptable, but stealing from someone's art was not. Although she did fall into the trap and use one of Leonard's lines in one of her songs.

Their boudoir, however, was productive in more than just a sexual sense; for both Cohen and Joni, relationships, love, were the very stuff of inspiration for their art. He introduced her to literature to help fill the gap in her education that she now felt keenly, especially as her lover would read Frederica Lorca, Albert Camus, Rainer Maria Rilke, the I Ching and the Zen masters. Whatever her thoughts, wrongly and rightly about his work, his music penetrated her, influenced her, and made her reassess her own songwriting. He inspired her, too, which she acknowledged.

'Marcie' is supposedly one such song, the lyrics influenced by Leonard Cohen she maintained, adding that without 'Suzanne', Marcie' would never have been written. Perhaps she was still in enamoured with Cohen's style phase. Yet, Marcie was still

written in her own inimitable style; she had thrown over the conventional song structure; she employed repetition for heightened effect and the dissection of ideas, saturated tones gushing from the clarity of her voice laying emotion bare.

The admiration was not simply one-sided, however, as Cohen admits to watching in astonishment as the girl whose beauty he found "compelling" adjusted her guitar to produce unheard of harmonies, and by the "fertility and abundance of her artistic enterprise", which he considered "more vast and varied... than the way I looked at things."

Joni thought that Leonard's song Bird on the Wire was about her, as she had shown him a painting she had done with sparrows sitting on a wire and one of them is upside down; the misfit, Joni, Cohen's "radiant presence", a woman whose physical effect on him was more important to him at the time than the music.

They collaborated musically, although Cohen knew that as far

as her writing was concerned she was her own master, but they explored the deeper caverns of emotion together and wrangled over lyrics until Joni had absorbed all that she could and they abandoned their lives as lovers forever.

The relationship with Leonard Cohen was not uncomplicated; she never found it easy to talk to him, thought him to be distant. She would ask questions in an attempt to move the relationship along only to be answered with "Oh Joni, you ask such beautiful questions" – questions to which she never received an answer. As the years passed, they saw each other less and less, until one day, she reported, he stopped talking to her almost altogether, repeating only "Joni, they'll never get us".

Joni's manager, Elliot Roberts was an important connection, for he was friends with David Geffen, and eventually he managed to get a recording contract with Reprise Records, one of only two deals that Joni had been offered. It was "the worst deal in the world" she recalled, but it was a deal.

Joni could have recorded three albums with the material she had, but she held back some of the best to reveal to the world as her career progressed, and some of her best songs did not fit thematically on the album. There was also a technical hiccup; her ex-lover David Crosby, formally of the Byrds, who Joni had

met in Miami in 1967, had devised a method for Joni to sing into a grand piano to have her voice reverberate. Unfortunately, the concept was incomplete, and imperfections were made worse in postproduction, which removed the high end of the vocals. Nonetheless, Song to a Seagull is an extraordinary debut album, which contains songs such as Marcie and Michael from the Mountains. In keeping with the times of Sgt Pepper innovation, the two sides of her album were called Part 1, I Came to the City, and Part 2, Out of the City and Down to the Seaside, to lend them a hint of sophistication.

The concluding track was Cactus Tree, written from Joni's experience of men, about a woman with many lovers who never match her expectations and who are left behind by her desire for freedom. Prophetic indeed.

Although she wasn't going to sell a great many albums, Joni radiated out into the world on her Seagull, and the unsuspecting world, including Rolling Stone journalists, were charmed, if not awestruck, by the "fresh, incredibly beautiful innocent/ experienced girl/woman".

Despite the imperfections of her debut album, her journey to fame, which would bypass stardom, had begun.

RIGHT:
Joni Mitchell, strumming her guitar outside The Revolution club in London, 1968

MAIN IMAGE:
Judy Collins and Joni Mitchell "back stage"
(around the swimming pool), Judy playing her
guitar, and Joni with chin in hand, listening.
Big Sur Hot Springs, 1968

MAIN IMAGE:
Graham Nash, Joni Mitchell, Nancy Carlen,
John Sebastian, Stephen Stills and Joan Baez
perform on stage during the 1968 Big Sur Folk
Festival at the Eselan Institute on September
8-9

GOLDEN YEARS

Following the release of her debut album, Joni went off on tour and gradually acquired a cult following. Several of her songs had been covered by other artists, so the music world eagerly awaited the release of her second album, Clouds. She often sang in the folk clubs on Bleecker Street in New York, where eager fans would crowd in to see her at the Cafe Au Go Go.

She had developed a habit of singing to one person that she could see in the audience to help anchor the song and give it focus; the intimacy of her songs, her idiosyncratic tunings, the "squeaky girl" voice, as she described it, the emotional availability, gentle yet raw, produced an electrifying effect in those who heard her.

After a harrowing experience with producer Paul Rothschild on the recording of the first track of the new album, Angel, Joni persuaded engineer Henry Lewy to help her record the rest of the album whilst Rothschild was away producing The Doors. Lewy agreed and became the de facto producer on the record. From then on, the singer would come to loathe the word producer, those who were an "interior decorator for people who are lazy or not full artists" was her caustic analysis. She was becoming more and more antagonistic about chauvinistic male treatment towards her and less and less inclined to pander to it. She knew that she was in a better position than anyone to produce her songs the way she wished them to be produced, and the only way to do that was to maintain control over all that she did.

Henry, therefore, was a godsend, an excellent engineer and modest as a man, and between them they worked through songs such as Chelsea Morning, The Gallery and Both Sides, Now in which Joni moved through fantasy and reality, love and losing love, emotional highs and lows even the occult; shades of Leonard Cohen.

Chelsea Morning, although she did not think it her best work, has become an iconic Joni Mitchell song. It's a good example of the strength of her visual sense expressed in words, of her facility and imagery, as she describes her small room in Chelsea, New York City.

Clouds, like Seagull, had a cover with a self-portrait that was designed and painted by Joni, as she fed her painting into her music in a blend that continued throughout her career. It was released on the 1st of May 1969, and its reviews were mixed; "Joni's voice sounds malnourished", despite "three excellent songs – "Roses Blue", "Both Sides, Now" and "Chelsea Morning".

Judy Collins won a 1969 Grammy award for Both Sides, Now, but the album could only manage a number 31 on the American Billboard 200 chart.

The "elegant bohemian princess" as David Yaffe described her, moved out to California along with Elliot Roberts and David Geffen, and into a house at 8217 Lookout Mountain Avenue in Laurel Canyon. It was a retreat from the hurly-burly of 1969 that she had so badly wanted, the place where she could live a domesticated life again, yet Sunset Boulevard could be reached in a five-minute drive.

Joni filled the house with "peace and love, art and poetry" according to Roberts. It became a magnet for the musical

MAIN IMAGE:

Photo shoot for the fashion magazine Vogue, 1968

glitterati, the place where Crosby, Stills and Nash saw the light of day. It was the place that gave birth to her first New York Times profile in which she expounded on her technique and art, about how she would sometimes write her words as poems and set them to music, about how writing music was like entering a trance and that in the future, she would like to record a song in the studio as soon as it was written.

Graham Nash stayed in Joni's house - she and he were almost in a state of marriage in Joni's eyes, and by the end of the relationship he considered her a musical genius.

Joni had to leave the happy domesticity of California to perform at two major events in 1969.

To start with she gave her first solo concert in New York's Carnegie Hall. The venue was bursting at the seams, her songs transported the audience and New York was in love with Joni Mitchell.

The second was supposed to have been at Woodstock, where Crosby, Stills, Nash and Young were playing, but which David Geffen caused her to miss by refusing to attend, although, inspired by this mass outpouring of love for music and the bitter disappointment at missing what she thought of as a "modern miracle", Joni composed the song Woodstock, a romantic eye cast over an event that forces musicians to become grotesque with effort and riddled with "backstage neuroses", as she put it. It was a song that could cause her to become overemotional to the extent that during her first few performances of it she had to stop singing in the middle of it. Perhaps, she ruminated, "it's because I didn't go to Woodstock but watched it on television", where she was moved to see how people would help each other out, sharing their food and delivering babies in the mud.

The day after the festival came her first appearance on national TV on the Dick Cavett show - where she was somewhat

bemused to be sharing the audience with bands who had been 'allowed' to play at Woodstock. And although she sang four songs, it proved hard for her to get a word in edgeways afterwards as the others enthused about the festival. Which was what the show was supposed to be about after all.

Joni regretted missing the event for a long time afterwards, crying when she sang her own powerful tribute to Woodstock; "We are stardust. We are golden. And we've got to get ourselves back to the garden". A garden that Joni knew was as temporal as the festival itself. The song was an astounding compaction of all that Woodstock was intended to represent, especially as it had been written by a woman who wasn't even there.

And then it was all over and she and Graham were back in California, back to domestication, to painting for Joni and photography for Graham, an enthusiasm that he later passed on to his lover.

They created happy memories in the house during that time together, but the patterns eventually repeated themselves; mental space was needed to create, and Graham moved on when love died, harbouring a special song that he had written, which would always remind him of their beautiful times together; Our House; a house which Joni also left a few years later.

For her part, Joni produced an album from that creative fountain at the house that marked another phase in her musical progress.

Released in April 1970, Ladies of the Canyon contained three of her greatest hits; Big Yellow Taxi, Woodstock and The Circle Game, and ushered in the era of Joni the commercial songstress. She played the piano for the first time on an album, running down the paths it opened for her to explore with a new freedom, to explore love, the environment, how life is lived. In doing so, she created lines that not only reflected the sentiments of the time but

RIGHT:
Celebration At Big Sur film poster, released in 1971

Celebrate with:
JOAN BAEZ
CROSBY, STILLS, NASH & YOUNG
JONI MITCHELL
JOHN SEBASTIAN
And Introducing
DOROTHY MORRISON
Everyone did it... for the sheer love of it.

CELEBRATION AT BIG SUR

...it happened one weekend by the sea.

Ted Mann Productions presents a film by Baird Bryant & Johanna Demetrakas
Produced by Carl Gottlieb Released by 20th Century-Fox COLOR by DE LUXE

71/144

became iconic in themselves; "They've paved paradise and put up a parking lot", from Big Yellow Taxi. And, of course, there was the song Willy, harking back to the days when love had been rich with Graham Nash and it had broken her heart to refuse his offer of marriage because her personal freedom was at stake; "If you try to hold sand too tightly, it slips through your fingers" she wrote to him from Crete in the spring 1970, where she had gone to take a break from touring, where she lived in a cave and became involved in a relationship with Canadian cook Cary Raditz.

"I loved the man", she would say of Nash in later years, and he, almost alone amongst their contemporaries, was never a target for her attacks for many, many years after. My Old Man was another song that she wrote about Nash.

The reviews spoke of her "richer, more sophisticated songs", that were "more compelling musically" than her previous work, of "direct poetry reminiscent of Leonard Cohen's", of her "Crystal clear imagery... shining bright as ever... a growingly powerful singer", and it is now seen as a transition work expanding her artistic horizons, leading to the more sophisticated albums of later years.

Ladies went to number 27 on the Billboard 200.

It was 1970, Joni was 26 years old, was voted "Top Female Performer" for 1970 by Melody Maker magazine, and she went to Alaska for a benefit concert to support Greenpeace, then in its early days. It was there that she came into contact with her next musical soulmate and lover, James Taylor, then 22 years old.

Taylor was also smitten by this "goddess of love", as he called her, and they were soon performing more venues together. They seemed to be in perfect harmony with one another, James writing You Can Close Your Eyes about her, which appeared on his 1971 Mud Slide Slim and the Blue Horizon album on which Joni sang backing vocals; yet the fractures lay below the surface in each of their characters. Taylor's ruptures were more imminent, and as they became an unavoidable reality in the shape of drugs and depression, Joni held him for as long as she could without descending into the abyss with him. "But I can sing this song, and you can sing this song when I'm gone" wrote Taylor prophetically.

MAIN IMAGE:
Photo shoot for the fashion magazine Vogue, 1968

Songs that she composed during this period are infused with lyrics of disturbed depth; the least that might emerge from such wrenching emotional experiences.

1970 was also the year that she played at the Isle of Wight festival to 600,000 people, and which she remembered with less than affection, recalling that "it was just horrible to play there". She called the concertgoers the "hate the artist" audience, and found herself in what she felt to be a fight or flight situation, about to do a concert alone on a huge stage. She hadn't wanted to see the audience and had chosen a night spot but was cajoled into taking an earlier one, at a time when the audience was rowdy. She calmed them, she said, with the knowledge she had gained from watching a Hopi snake dance in the desert.

With James still at her side, and Joni deeply invested in the relationship, Joni embarked on what has now become recognised as one of the greatest albums of all time, one of the "turning points and pinnacles in 20th-century popular music" as the New York Times wrote; Blue.

Songs inspired by Crete and Cary Radnitz, by Graham Nash and by James, of course, found their way onto the album with its stark blue cover in which Joni stripped her emotions bare and bound them up in multi-octave vocal runs supported by forceful open chords. This simplified, rhythmic, acoustic focus allowed Joni's voice and emotions the space to have a more direct impact on the listener. "I felt like I had absolutely no secrets from the world and I couldn't pretend in my life to be strong" she said of the album.

It was a dangerous place for her to be when she was tripping; she took an overdose of acid that intensified all of the wounded, frightened emotions that she harboured about the world. Her strange dreams were fed by years of pent-up sadness, by loss; she cried at the slightest provocation. An inability to cope with the demands of fame, which she experienced as an intense pressure to be something she didn't want to be – whatever that was – and which she realised was making her become unstable. Her condition became so fragile that the recording sessions for Blue had to be locked off, inaccessible for others. They produced songs like River, thought to be inspired by Nash, about a girl losing

MAIN IMAGE:
Photo shoot for the fashion magazine Vogue, 1968

MAIN IMAGE:
Joni Mitchell live at the Isle Of Wight Festival,
August 29th 1970

HAROLD LEVENTHAL PRESENTS
AT CARNEGIE HALL

AN HOUR WITH

JOAN BAEZ

THURSDAY EVE. FEBRUARY 11th 1971

2 PERFORMANCES – ONE HOUR PROGRAM
NO INTERMISSION
AT 7:15 P.M. AND 9:30 P.M.
ALL SEATS RESERVED $2.00

JONI MITCHELL

SATURDAY EVE. FEBRUARY 13th 1971
AT 8:40 P. M.

TICKETS: $5.00, 4.50, 3.75, 3.00

Tickets Now on Sale at Carnegie Hall Box Office Only

her lover, realising that blame is a two-step; "I'm so hard to handle, I'm selfish and I'm sad, now I've gone and lost the best baby, that I ever had". Joni solo on piano at her most confessional, circling around universal emotions, engaged in a never-ending tug of war.

Blue changed the path of love songs, love was now a two-edged sword that in Joni's world often scythed the bearer. Blue was her final farewell, almost, to the flowery happiness of the love ever after of popular culture. Joni's love hurt. Blue might well be seen as Joni opening her soul wider than ever before, baring her scars, confessing her excesses, and people were shocked.

Those who heard Blue heard the singer's pain very clearly and worried about her. Kris Kristofferson said, "Oh, Joni. Save something of yourself." As always, however, her indomitable spirit can also be heard on an album that drags the listener through brooding, through sorrow, through happiness, implosion and cascades of love. On the classic track A Case of You, often considered to be referring to Graham Nash, she writes,

"...go to him, stay with him if you can
Oh, but be prepared to bleed
Oh, but you are in my blood you're my holy wine
Oh, and you taste so bitter, bitter and so sweet
Oh, I could drink a case of you darling
Still I'd be on my feet.

Joni wasn't giving in, she was defiant, she was exorcising, she was exuberant, she was depressed.

Having criticised the pop industry for its black and white vision of love, she presented its panoramic effervescence, but in such an intimate fashion that the album was, she said, like "private letters that were published". And the singer turned the screw by insisting that people related the songs to their own lives and did not simply "rubberneck" her experiences. The endearing mélange of emotional vulnerabilities helped the album to eventually sell over 10 million copies, despite scepticism

LEFT:
Poster advertises Carnegie Hall concerts, two performances by Joan Baez and one by Joni Mitchell, New York, New York, February 1971

about its commercial viability at the time. It rose to number three in Britain and number 15 in the US.

Having splashed her emotional life onto the pavement in Blue, distrusting of almost everyone she met, Joni retreated northwards back to her homeland and the light-reflecting sea of British Columbia in western Canada. Here she bought 160 acres of land, also buying two neighbouring properties to ensure her privacy, built a house without electricity, which she thought would make her ill, a little stone house "like a monastery where I could just go away and hide". It was a period in her life when money and success appeared distasteful to her, disproportionate rewards for what she was doing. She would cry at the slightest emotional tremor inside herself, and her impression of the world and the future that it was heading towards horrified her. She would have visions of the Earth being destroyed. She remembers that she even cried when the estate agents took her around British Columbia to show her plots of land.

When she finally found her home, she fully intended to stay there forever, enchanted by the birds, the rainbows and the magic of the land itself. She fashioned the interior to reflect her interior life, removed herself from the world outside, inviting only friends into her womb when she felt the need of company. One of those allowed access was Tony Simon, a friend from her adolescence, someone she could trust and who inevitably became her lover – and a life-long confidante; another was Leonard Cohen. Joni never wanted enemies in place of ex-lovers.

She buried herself in books on psychology and theology and especially in the works of Nietzsche, who seem to offer a way out of the turmoil she experienced, by suggesting that as living equates to suffering then finding meaning in that suffering is a way to keep living. She sought the pearl in the oyster of her depression, accepting the dark side of life as the source of her inspiration. "Without music, life would be a mistake" was a line from Nietzsche that would have resonated strongly within her.

LEFT:

Protester named Yogi Joe interrupting Joni Mitchell's performance at the Isle of Wight Festival 1970

In an interview, Joni replied to a question about the philosopher Nietzsche. "There's a lot of Nietzsche in my songs" she replied, going on to say that the main thing that she had garnered from him was support. In the same way that he was pointing out how Germany was decaying, she was commenting on America's decay.

When she came across a study of the Beethoven, she felt that she had discovered another misunderstood musician like herself, ringed in with self-doubt, desperate to discover if there was a person inside that people would like.

The piano in the little house outside of Vancouver began to fill the air with music as she wrestled with her biggest composition to date, which eventually bore the name Judgment of the Moon

and Stars, inspired by Beethoven, the rebel with whom she could identify, whose music also broke with convention. And she could see her own destiny in his, the man losing his abilities, raging against his deafness, falling silent.

From this sense of running a race only to lose in the end anyway, would come the title of her next album, For the Roses, and Beethoven was added to a growing list of musicians and artists of the highest rank with whom she felt an affinity and equality. They had striven until the very end, and she would, too.

RIGHT:
Joni Mitchell, posed, with zither

MAIN IMAGE:
Joni Mitchell talks to Carole King in the control room of A&M Records Recording Studio during the recording of King's album 'Tapestry' in January 1971

CHANGING HER TUNE

If Joni had followed her inner voice, the voice of the country girl longing for the carefree open vistas of the countryside when she abandoned California for British Columbia. Yet she discovered that she could not live without the tumbling turmoil of life in the city, and within a year she was back in California, staying with David Geffen.

But it was in New York that the applause at Carnegie Hall in 1972, when Joni played her new songs there on the 23rd of February, almost raised the roof. Many of the songs would appear on her new album that she had worked on in the quietness of British Columbia, where she produced compositions that reflected a world very different to that around her little stone house. A world where drugs were increasingly prevalent, the Vietnam War raged on and traditional values were being trashed. The freedom of the north she brought to her record on the album inside cover, which reveals her nakedness against the backdrop of Canadian waters near her home, whilst the outside cover showed her tanned and sitting beside the sea.

Her performance brought in plaudits for the greater range of her articulation, the dark chest tones and the "aesthetic density of the music" from a woman who the New York Times considered as possibly "one of the most genuinely gifted composers North America has yet developed".

When the album was released eight months after the Carnegie Hall concert, critical acclaim came flooding in; "She's a songwriter and singer of genius who can't help but make us feel we are not alone" enthused the New York Times. "As literate a

MAIN IMAGE:

Joni Mitchell posed in Amsterdam, Holland in 1972

writer as we have (who) continues to produce works of richness and value", opined the Los Angeles Times.

They were speaking of songs such as the title track, For the Roses, beautifully structured, relating to her dissatisfaction with the media circus that she so hated and that was very soon to engulf her completely. The signs were already there; the album For the Roses contained the hit single "You Turn Me On, I'm a Radio", which was Joni being sarcastic because David Geffen had asked her for a song that was radio friendly. By now she had signed to Asylum Records, which had been founded by David Geffen and Elliot Roberts, and Geffen wanted help to get the new company up and running. Ironically, the song reached number 25 on the Billboard Hot 100 charts, which made it her first top 40 hit.

Other songs are reportedly references to her relationship with James Taylor and her distraught state of mind after their breakup. There is confrontation, there is anger, there is defiance in abundance to emotionally exhaust even the most avid listener. The avid listener would also hear Joni's continual growing pains, her ability to explore a variety of emotional perspectives, as Rolling Stone stated, and also the truth according to Joni, a woman who was unconventional, fractured and defiantly needy, but supremely gifted. They would also hear a re-tuning of her personal musical direction, which would flourish in her next album, Court and Spark.

Gradually, the wider world with which she maintained such a fraught and suspicious relationship began to raise her up to the level of her male peers. The grandeur of her lyrics, the sophistication of music and tunings, her changed voice that had ripened and gained depth, brought her compositions onto a different plane, away from the musings of a young woman, turning the personal and intimate into the universal.

Court and Spark was another step away from the vulnerable, sweet country girl image that seemed to have lodged in the

LEFT:
Joni Mitchell during an interview, Amsterdam, 1972

55

MAIN IMAGE:

Joni Mitchell during an interview, Amsterdam, 1972

JONI MITCHELL

MAIN IMAGE:
Joni Mitchell draws listeners from other performing areas at the Mariposa Folk Festival on the Islands, 1972

musical airwaves. Using a band for the first time, drawing from the extra force that it brought, was another way of distancing herself from that image.

Yet vulnerable she remained, vulnerable to the intrusion of audiences into her consciousness if she had not submerged herself completely into her songs on stage; "... if anything happened in the room, if there was a flutter or something, it would be a distraction to me". That distraction might cause her to stop singing altogether and tell the audiences that she could not continue with the song. It was not unknown for her to even leave the stage completely.

In California, where every second Hollywood star seemed to be lying on a psychiatrist's couch, Joni found herself talking to renowned German psychoanalyst Doctor Martin Grotjahn. She had much to investigate, not least the areas scattered with so many broken relationships and heartbreak. But the psychoanalyst's patients seemed to know one another and talk about each other to him, as in the case of Warren Beatty, another of the Joni's would-be lovers, as was Jack Nicholson,

and everyone, including the psychologist, seemed to become obsessed with her. For a woman in the throes of confusion and deep sadness, the sessions were leading in the wrong direction, taking her downwards into darkness instead of upwards into the air.

Joni, it seemed, was not sparing the rod on herself, for she also found herself in a relationship with Jackson Browne, whose own mother warned Joni against starting a relationship with him. It was a short-lived union, brought about when they were on tour together, although she insisted that she loved, with the coda "to the best of my abilities", whilst believing that he had never been attracted to her. But in the precarious mental state in which Joni found herself at time, the ultimate rejection by Browne inevitably caused enormous damage to her. Not least because her ego could not abide being rejected, resulting in her lashing out bitterly afterwards. Jackson Browne was reduced to a "leering narcissist", although it must be said that he, too, was a fractured personality. Perhaps she needed those troubled men so that she could pin them to the wall like butterflies and examine them under her microscope, where she might find the answers to her

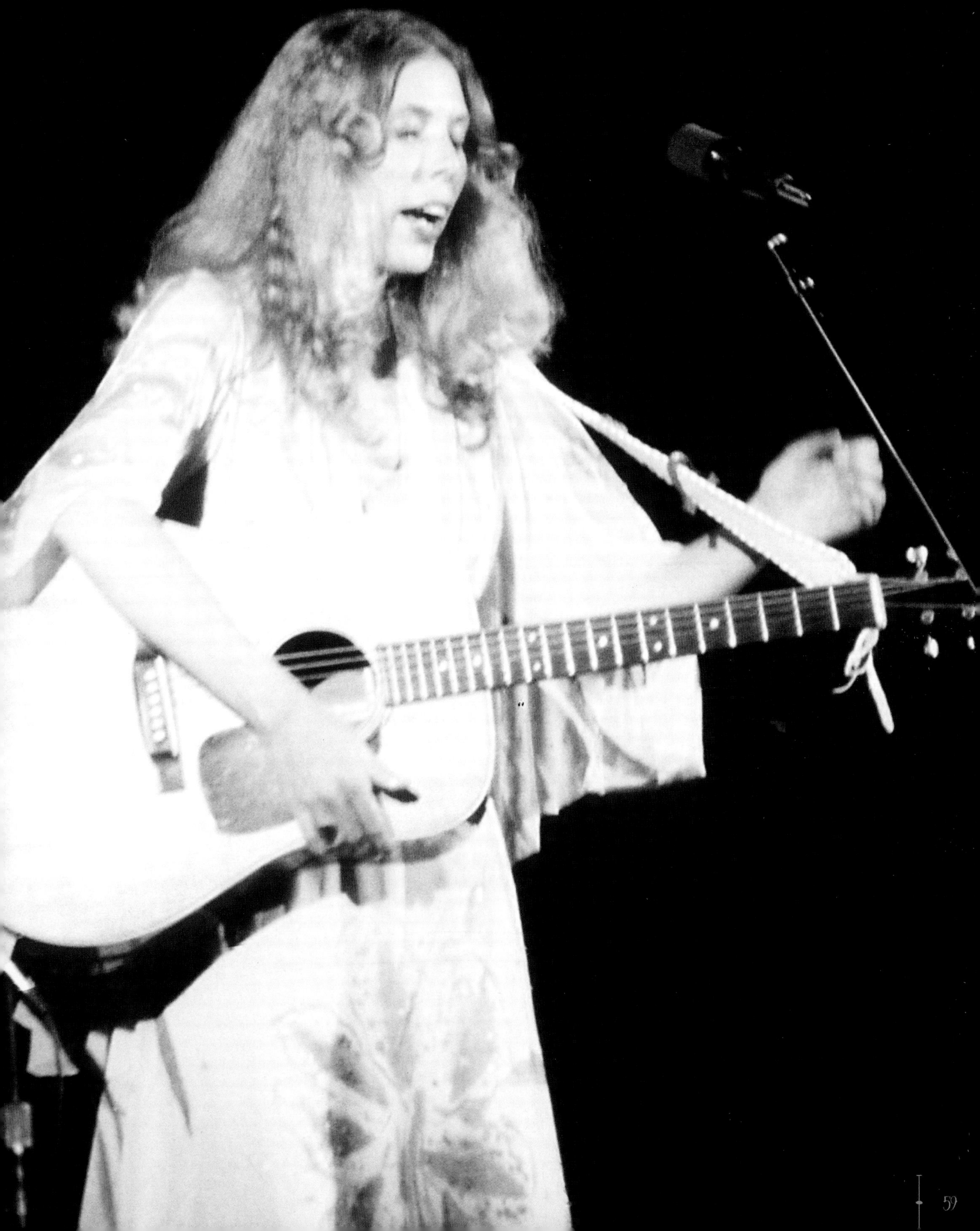

own urging questions, her own life that could seem like nothing but splintered glass, a compass with endless magnetic north points. Joni enjoyed the company of men, enjoyed that they considered her to be one of the boys. Even though she felt they lacked imagination, she enjoyed their camaraderie, so unlike the "conspiratorial" girls she had found in her young years.

Jackson wrote Fountain of Sorrow, which was ostensibly his heartbreak anthem, after his relationship with Joni Mitchell collapsed.

Rumours surfaced that Joni was suicidal, which she denied, but already she was moving on to new conquests. One of them was the drummer for L. A. Express, a jazz pop ensemble, one of the leading proponents of the jazz-rock style and most prolific drummers of his era. His name was John Guerin, and he would become a door to another enticing musical path, opening her ears and eyes to see how she could realign her lonely musical journey, stride in a new direction. They would spend many hours in bed listening to jazz and enjoying a relationship that took her through another album and subsequent tour.

MAIN IMAGE:
Joni Mitchell records her album "Court And Spark" at A&M Recording Studios on La Brea Avenue with John Guerin on drums and Larry Carlton on guitar in 1973 in Hollywood, California

That album would be Court and Spark, her most successful album; she was joined by Guerin, bassist Max Bennett, Joe Sample on keyboards and Tom Scott on reeds. Joni was saying goodbye to her folk roots without a glance behind. These were all seasoned musicians, with jazz techniques second to none, who were all mature enough to serve the music and not their own egos and who had no problem following Joni's unnamed chord progressions. Lead guitarist John Carlton added indelibly to the mix with his volume pedal with which he could sustain either chords or notes, introducing a musical ambience that pleased Joni and complimented her own rhythmic strumming.

It all gelled to produce a stunning album filled with lightness and introducing songs about love's illusions and seductions, as in the title track, for example. In Rolling Stone, the reviewer mused that there was also a darkness to the album, because "No thought or emotion is expressed without some equally forceful statement of its negation. Joni Mitchell", he went on "seems destined to remain in a state of permanent dissatisfaction - always knowing what she would like to do, always more depressed when it's done".

Court and Spark was a concept album in which Joni delved again into the interplay of honesty and trust in romantic and platonic relationships. She had entered the field of the character study as in A Free Man in Paris, a song about David Geffen relaxing in the City of Light with her and another friend. Geffen did not want the song to be published, as he was gay and terrified of the backlash. She did not listen.

But of course without self-doubt and worry it would not be a Joni Mitchell work, and The Same Situation, with Joni wondering about loneliness on her "search for love that don't seem to cease", and People's Parties, take off along those paths. So typical of Joni to question everything and thereby run the risk of denuding everything of its value. Maybe she wrote these songs about Warren Beatty with whom she was friendly at the time. His was a complex ego much like her own - David Crosby describing

her as "about as modest as Mussolini" - a palette filled with bright colours for her brush.

Her fears about her own psyche are aired in songs about madness, such as the final two offerings, which approach the subject from different angles. In Trouble Child, tragedy is the medium of expression, whilst in Lambert, Hendricks & Ross's Twisted (for Joni as a high school student, the group were her equivalent of the Beatles, the sound of liberation) is "a piece of comedy with a hilarious punch line that plays on the very notion of schizophrenia". Together they "flirt with insanity from a distance safe enough to show she can control even so threatening a concern", in the words of Rolling Stone.

The drifter in "Court And Spark" tells of a casual affair and the lover who tries to protect herself by not investing too heavily in the relationship - something she finds herself unable to do in Help Me, Joni's only top 10 single, where her will has failed and the result is love that is threatening rather than pleasant, love that she must grin and bear rather than yield to willingly. An abstract freedom is always worth more than the fear of the unworthy self in a Joni Mitchell relationship. "Flirting and flirting, hurting, too, we love our lovin', but not like we love our freedom". So she moves on and tries to avoid the frenzy of love: "I used to count lovers like railroad cars, I counted them on my side, lately I don't count nothing, I just let things slide", she sings on Just Like This Train, before revealing more about herself: "This jealous lovin's bound to make me crazy, I can't find my goodness, I lost my heart, oh, sour grapes, because I just lost my heart".

Court and Spark would rise to number two on the Billboard charts selling over 2 million copies in its first year. Joni Mitchell had become a household name. Her answer to the question what did she think of her newfound fame was evasive; she had never expected to become so well known, was all she would reveal. Others were not so circumspect, expressing the opinion that Joni's music, containing as it did lyrical excellence and musical

mastery, would still be holding its ground in 200 years time.

Perhaps for the first time in her career, Joni had become a popular act. She went out on tour with the album in January 1974, travelling across the United States and Canada for two months, receiving rave notices. She played in large halls and college campuses and debuted two new songs, Jericho and Love or Money, the latter finding the singer musing about the point in her life she has arrived at and about the firmament of Tinsel Town, about striving and failing; "Vaguely she floats and lace-like, blown in like a curtain on the night wind, she's nebulous and naked".

The concerts at the Universal Amphitheatre in Los Angeles between August the 14th and the 17th, which were filled to capacity at the 5200-seat venue, were recorded and became a two-record set with almost all of the songs from the concert. The album was called Miles of Aisles and eventually equalled the success of Court and Spark, reaching number two on the Billboard charts.

Joni's music resonated in the hearts and minds of her listeners, giving them the comfort of knowing that they weren't alone, that she had been scythed by life and love and that she was still standing, still fighting, still loving, and the music was beginning to influence everyone who heard it.

But now that the tentacles of commercial success were enfolding her, what effect would it have on the rebel girl, who, "having had a small taste of success, and having seen the consequences of what it gives to you and what it takes away in terms of what you think it's going to give you", now had the industry licking its lips. For the moment, she simply wanted to take her music on the road with musicians she respected. L. A. Express opened for her and stood behind her when she played, whilst other musicians joined and left again. And although the open chords presented no problem to these professionals,

Joni's unexpected chordal changes of direction meant that there could be no slacking in concentration by the musicians providing the accompaniment.

By September the 2nd 1974 when the tour ended in Boulder, Joni had played seventy-five dates and faced the biggest audiences she had ever attracted. Her love affair with John Guerin had the temperature on full, and the pair lived together and could not be parted; success and money were hers. It was a sweet period in Joni's life.

But as ever with the chameleon singer, change was in the air, and she was moving away fast, certainly from folk, but also from her newly found jazz-pop towards using a wider range of instruments in jazz-inspired songs. She wondered how long David Geffen and the record companies would play ball if you could not roll out the big dollars with each album, but such considerations were never at the forefront of her mind; the music directed her on the search for her own truth.

Since the end of the tour, she had been writing new material, and early in 1975 she went into the studio. When she emerged again it would be with her new album, The Hissing of Summer Lawns.

It was as though she had not only changed musical direction but also the direction of her ire, for she launched her arrows directly at the bourgeois chattering classes, the hollowness of genteel bohemia, in fact anyone that she suspected of shallowness. Which was most of the people around her, it seemed, in the new genteel life that she inhabited. The songs illuminated a sense of being trapped, of not being master of your own destiny, the characters, most of whom are women, have lost connection to their innermost feelings.

Speaking some time afterwards, she thought that women, in particular, found the songs confrontational because they were

not sung in the first person, no longer simply about the singer herself. She was, she said, holding up a mirror and her listeners didn't like what they saw; they wanted to keep their struggles safely at arm's length, safely in Joni's world.

There is no ambiguity in the long verse structures constructed to tie in with speech rhythms. These were not the same genre of heartbreak songs that Blue gave to the world; these observations were more wide-ranging, broader than anything that had gone before. She had, as one reviewer noted, "done little work on her melodies… she is up to something too subtle for me to detect". The musicians had been allowed more leeway, the free-form electric piano, for example, because Joni was fully aware that a jazz musician left to his own devices would play against her melodies.

The title track was a collaboration with John – working with him brought her immense joy, and she recalls falling in love with him doing a performance of the track Harry's House – which immediately shows the way for the album to proceed with "a barbed-wire fence to keep out the unknown, and on every metal thorn just a little blood of his own", whilst the man's lover "stays with a love of some kind, it's the lady's choice". And where did this loyalty lead? In Joni's eyes it led to Sweet Bird and "all these vain promises on beauty jars" as the earth spins and the sky rushes past and the singer lay down "golden in time and woke up vanishing". A sentiment very close to Joni's heart.

But some of her more stinging barbs were reserved for those around her doing the "old romance – the boho dance" in Boho Dance, those who were "like a priest with a pornographic watch, looking and longing on the sly", or in Edith and the Kingpin, an amalgam of a Vancouver pimp that Joni once met and Edith Piaf. In the song, Joni points up the mutual dependency that produces half characters temporarily locked together in time, and women discarded when they are no longer of use, which was Joni's cynical take on the music business; "… each with

charm to sway, are staring eye to eye, they dare not look away". In the hiatus before she went out on tour to promote the album, and the cold hand of cynicism that would separate Joni and John began to grip them, Joni found herself on the Rolling Thunder Revue tour with Bob Dylan from November the 30th until December the 8th and a concert at Madison Square Garden. Remembering Woodstock, she had been determined not to miss another of life's great experiences, although she avoided being filmed for the Renaldo and Clara film that Dylan and Sam Shepard made.

Joni considered Dylan to be someone to emulate and keep pace with; "I liked the more storytelling quality of Dylan's work and the idea of the personal narrative. He would speak as if to one person in a song… That was the key that opened all the doors". Leonard Cohen, was another 'pacemaker'. And as Dylan had been inspired by Joni's Blue album, a tour with Bob, in which she hoped to get closer to the singer, seemed to offer a tantalising experience. Which indeed, it did – alongside nightmarish ones.

Rolling Thunder, "coerced", was the word she used, and remembered Joan Baez coming to her door to make her stay on and complimenting her by saying that Joni had had the loudest applause. So Joni stayed and took cocaine, wrote her songs, was unable to sleep and became incredibly aggressive, stealing policeman's badges. Coyote is one song that was fuelled by coke – and by Sam Shepard, another admirer of the Canadian singer and her collages of words and "unique jazz structures". He was married and had another lover on the tour, but of course, the two became entwined in romance – what did a marriage matter between friends. "Sam and I had a flirtation" was how Joni put it, a "flirtation" fired by their intelligence and cocaine, a meeting of creative minds in love with words, although both knew it would end with the tour; "No regrets Coyote".

Joni and the Rolling Thunder Tour bid farewell to each other

LEFT:
Joni Mitchell, 1975

following her final concert the day after her prison episode. Just over one month later she was back on the road on her own tour.

It was mid-January 1976 when fans began to crowd into the halls to see Joni and hear her songs. On the 28th, they had Dylan as well; he joined her by way of a thank you for the Rolling Thunder Tour. Joni might have wished he hadn't done so, because she remembered him simply wandering around on the stage and acting very weirdly, although, they apparently performed Both Sides, Now together.

Not only that, the relationship with John was further strained, when he found Bob and Joni in a bedroom together (believe it or not, they'd been discussing God), overlooking the fact that their friend Boyd Elder was also there. Guerin immediately went out and bought himself female companionship, leading to an almighty row between John and Joni in their room later, which even became physical. The fights led to them continuing the tour but sleeping in separate rooms. Paradise was being paved over and she found herself catapulted back into one of her own songs.

This led to the difficult situation where Joni wished to continue working with John, and had no wish to prevent him from seeing other women, but insisted that they separate their spheres of activity; no more flights in the private plane with anyone else, no one else at the concerts, and any new woman would have to remain an unnamed secret in the background. John agreed – and promptly brought in a former girlfriend who, apparently,

looked just like Joni – and allowed her to fly in the plane and drive with them in Joni's limo – to which Joni said nothing. The situation was causing her pain, yet her complaints to Elliot Roberts fell on deaf ears.

And there were more problems with Gayle Ford, wife of her guitarist Robben, who turned out to be what Joni called a queen bee, and a "disruptive and megalomaniacal… nightmare" and caused the singer problems at every turn, even though Joni tried to help her and keep her on the tour.

There was worse to come.

On February the 22nd, she was due to play a concert at the University of Maryland. All the trauma of the breakup with John and the impossible peripheral circumstances that were crushing her self-esteem on the tour finally overwhelmed her. Even the sound check before the concert went against her, the sound echoing from the walls.

She made it onto the stage for the evening concert, managed to blurt out "Help me" and then rushed off the stage. The concert was cancelled, as was a planned European tour.

Joni would, for the most part, stay away from gigs in the future. She cared not for the money, or the men who lost money, she cared not for the disappointed fans; she cared about her own personal sanity.

LEFT:
Joni Mitchell and session musician John Guerin in studio circa 1976 in Los Angeles, California

MAIN IMAGE:

**Joni Mitchell performs live on stage watched by
Stephen Stills at Wembley Stadium, London on
14th September 1974**

THE DRUNK WITH SAGE'S EYES

When the Hissing of the Lawns album came out in November 1975, the incomprehension of the many was balanced by the admiration of the few such as Prince or Elvis Costello ("a misunderstood masterpiece"), whose own songs were inspired by the album, and those more discerning would write "This is songwriting of the highest order, brimming with telling detail, yet pared to the bone, refined and yet teeming with suggestion", whilst for Rolling Stone the verdict was "a great collection of pop poems with a distracting soundtrack".

As 1975 moved over to make way for 1976, Joni could only move on in the direction she felt she had no choice but to go. She was planning her next album during the break following her collapsed concert tour; Hejira.

"I had an idea; I knew I wanted to travel. Hejira was an obscure word that said exactly what I wanted; running away, honourably. It dealt with the leaving of a relationship, but "without the sense of failure that accompanied the breakup of my previous relationships."

Hejira was to be her most experimental work to date, on which she collaborated with the virtuoso jazz bass guitarist Jaco Pastorious, and which, she said, "was written mostly while I was travelling in the car. That's why there were no piano songs".

She'd been on a road trip with two friends, one of them an ex-lover - she was a glutton for punishment it seemed; perhaps it was the cocaine she was still taking, even though it destroyed the heart, she said. Many of her songs were fuelled by cocaine at this time; it kept her confidence and energy levels high. Don Juan's Reckless Daughter, Song for Sharon, a song with no bridge, no chorus and ten verses long, or Talk to Me, all owe their origins to cocaine. Already a "chicken squawkin'", her words, she became even more loquacious on coke.

Now she was heading for Maine and had taken off with the boys with the words "I've been waiting for you. I'm gone".

She embarked on three road trips between 1975 and 1976, trips that took her from Los Angeles to Maine, to California via Florida and the Gulf of Mexico. She would stay in lighthouses on the coast; in New Orleans she disguised herself by wearing wigs and sunglasses. "I pass through some seedy town with a pinball arcade, fall in with people who work on the machines, people staying alive shoplifting, whatever, they don't know who you are". She would tell them that her name was Joan Black. As she had no driver's license, she drove only during the day, staying with convoys of truckers, who signalled when the police were up ahead of them.

She went to stay with her former guitarist Robben Ford. It was a fortuitous meeting, because he had a copy of Jaco Pastorius's new album. Jaco was her kind of musician, one who would leave her the space to play that she was desperate for, whilst weaving his own inventive brilliance around her. He, too, was breaking new ground in his field; a perfect match. Whilst maintaining absolute precision rhythm playing, he elicited sounds from the bass that it had never made before, as though it had gone beyond its own range, gave the impression that more than one person was playing, seducing the treble notes as no one before had done. It was this man that she heard on Portrait of Tracy, and it felt as though her dream had become reality; she had found a man refusing to accept the boundaries presented to him, even removing the frets from the neck of his instrument in the attempts to hunt down the sounds that he wanted, and she knew she wanted him on her next album.

What she also found indirectly through Robben Ford was a Tibetan Buddhist Master, ironically introduced to her by Gayle Ford, her nemesis from The Hissing of Summer Lawns tour. His name was Vidyadhara Chögyam Trungpa Rinpoche, thought to be a reincarnated lama, an exile from the Chinese invasion and now working at Naropa University in Boulder. Having bypassed eastern philosophy in a younger years, she was now ripe for help from somewhere outside of her own sphere of activity.

Like an angry schoolchild, she belligerently took a cocaine hit in front of him on the first meeting, as though she were afraid of what was to come; the confrontation with herself, of experiencing the "pain of seeing ourselves" as one of Trungpa's students would say. Having been introduced by Gayle Ford, Joni became condescending to him, but had underestimated her sparring partner.

Trungpa seemed an odd choice for a woman trying to get her life into some semblance of order, because the monk did not present a traditional image of a Buddhist monk. He was a heavy drinker, in fact he died of alcoholism, and would have affairs with his female students. And yet he had the ability to whittle away the defensive constructs that his students used to keep their fears at bay, to deal with what frightened them.

Joni was lucid enough to understand that something great was being introduced into her life, and within fifteen minutes, her scaffolding had collapsed and her ego, inflated with handsome men, cocaine and compliments, had gone down with it. By the time she left his presence, "the drunk with sage's eyes" as he became to her many years later, she would think of him as a friend of the spirit, who drank and womanised. She was, she said, in "the awakened state". She spent three days in that state. "The thing you think you are is not there. But your full nature is there. There is nothing to report back to". In fact, as she put it, "your 'I' thing is gone". She would continue with her Buddhist studies and achieve level four Buddhism, the final of four stages of attainment.

MAIN IMAGE:
Joni Mitchell mid 1970s

At a concert in Wisconsin on February the 29th 1976, the photos for her new album were shot by a freezing Lake Mendota. Starkly clad in a black stole and woolly beret, she managed the shoot like her songs, with great precision and an eye for detail, to ensure the vivid black and white contrast would appear exactly as she desired. Joni had already laid down the basis of the tracks that would become the new album, Hejira, before she met Pastorius. Four of the tracks on the new album were overdubbed with his bass parts, and it is he and the singer that dominate the music.

This was Joni "running away honourably", in other words, leaving the relationship with John Guerin without the "sense of failure... it was not necessarily anybody's fault. It was a new attitude". This attitude was intended to push her music into different places, to stretch her, to achieve a sense of unity with the sophistication she desired in the music and the sophistication of her taste.

In Hejira, the personal revelations were back again in a different form. Joni felt that Hejira was a more accessible album and that people were more comfortable with it because the focus was back on her internal strife, on her trials and tribulations, and they preferred that to being confronted by their own. "People live vicariously" she said, "they didn't "want to really identify", see her problems as theirs, too.

"My friends were calling up all day yesterday, all emotions and abstractions, it seems we all live so close to that line, and so far from satisfaction" she sings in Song for Sharon

Joni thought the album really inspired, with a "restless feeling throughout it", infused with the bitter-sweetness of travelling alone, although she now had two soul mates on her journey; Jaco – the enormity of whose playing seems to ooze into the rest of the album, despite his presence on only four tracks; on Coyote, where his contribution to the open road aura is immeasurable; on the atmospheric title song Hejira; on Black Crow, with its guitar-heavy disorientation, and on Refuge of the Roads – and Trungpa, who helped Joni onto a new trajectory, into a new clarity.

Jaco and the other musicians never met in the studio; Joni was certain enough of their superior professionalism to use overdubs. And Jaco was a superb musician, propelling the album to another level with his rhythmic and harmonic support, using a soloist's melodic vistas, making what was difficult sooth into the ear like honey, as he added dramatic harmonics, caressing Joni's lyric as he, indeed, caressed the singer herself – for, yes, the two had become lovers; Coyote was now their song.

"Either he's going to have to stand and fight or take off out of here, I tried to run away myself, to run away and wrestle with my ego and with this flame you put here in this Eskimo, in this hitcher, in this prisoner of the five white lines, of the white lines on the free, free way."

Jaco was another bad boy, bipolar, his emotions rioting, his condition indistinguishable from and contributing to, his extraordinary talent, a soul in the same hemisphere as Joni, a human bullet speeding to destruction (and he ended up sleeping on park benches); she even wanted to have a child by him, knowing he was married. He already had children, he wanted no more complications. Music and sex were all he wanted from Joni. Once again, she had found a situation that she could not resist, one that would kick her and confirm what she thought she knew. So the contradictions could continue untarnished, as she sang in the title track Hejira: "We are only particles of change and I know, I know, orbiting around the sun, but how can I have that point of view, when I'm always bound and tied to someone". Caught in her own whirlpool of conflicting attractions, she could settle on none, and the ones she couldn't have, helped her flee to the next and preserve her abstract sense of freedom.

The song was difficult for Joni to write, as it sets out her reasons for leaving John Guerin, speaking of the incompatibility of love, professional life, freedom and belonging; "In our possessive coupling, so much could not be expressed, so now I'm returning to myself, these things that you and I suppressed".

Song for Sharon, Sharon being a childhood friend, is Joni looking back into a shrinking past to find pieces for her puzzle of the future. She sings to Sharon, letting her thoughts drift back to Canada, always confessing; "I came out to the Big Apple here, to face the dream's malfunction". She remembers her childhood, skating, remembering someone drowning, comparing domesticity with the "apple of temptation" that is her lot. Still, she concludes, she lives in hope of green pastures "by and by".

In Amelia, Joni is remembering again, remembering Amelia Earhart this time, another soul seeking wider horizons, overcoming boundaries and prejudices and the scathing male condescension that Joni knew so well; another female, ignoring what was set by convention, embracing what could be. "Like me, she had a dream to fly, like Icarus ascending on beautiful foolish arms". Now, a Joni free of drugs had found a soulmate, albeit 40 years too late, confessing to her woman to woman and musing that she finds that she's never really loved, that she has spent her whole life in clouds at an icy attitude. And what is left of the dream to fly they both harboured, metaphorically and in reality? Nothing but more dreams... and false alarms.

There's another comparison on Black Crow, where she relates to the bird that is diving down to pick up every shiny thing before flying back into the blue sky. But unlike the crow, the singer is not satisfied, for "in search of love and music, my whole life has been illumination, corruption" she sings on a fast-paced track on which Jaco is let loose to create his own distinct harmonics and rhythms free of drums, providing a sharp contrast to the lyric's sentiments.

It's John Guerin's memory that is still bothering her in the track Blue Motel Room, whilst the album's travails and trips through the singer's psyche finish with what Joni thought of as one of her favourite songs, Refuge of the Roads. She was thinking about her visit to Trungpa when she wrote the song about someone else that she had met and left for the refuge from the world that travelling brought, a refuge from those who she thought could not see what she saw. She abandoned the "heart and humour and humility" that Trungpa had wanted her to carry with her on her journey in her "baggage overload, westbound and rolling, taking refuge in the roads". Another Joni contradiction; it was on those roads that she enjoyed meeting the very people she sang were not on her wavelength, "regular folks"; but she enjoyed becoming an ordinary person and escaping what she had become. She found it difficult to adhere to Trungpa's Buddhist wisdom; but he had, at least, cleared the clouds of the past's wistful memories and allowed her a clearer view of her present.

RIGHT:

Joni Mitchell poses for portrait 1976 in Los Angeles, California

ROADS LESS TRAVELLED

I n November 1976, when Hejira was released to good reviews – "new seductive rhythms", "sophisticated and arresting as anything she's done", Joni was involved in another spectacular show, which went a little way in helping to plug the gap in her CV left by missing Woodstock. The American-Canadian group The Band was giving a farewell concert appearance; this was to be named The Last Waltz. Alongside The Band themselves, would be a potpourri of special guests including Eric Clapton, Neil Diamond, Dylan, Emmylou Harris, and Muddy Waters. Joni sang Coyote, Shadows and Light and Furry Sings the Blues accompanied by Neil Young on harmonica. Joni was the centre of everyone's affection, sharing a trailer with Neil Young, with whom she would also share harmonies on the song Acadian Driftwood, but still feeling somewhat lonely amongst the crowd. Martin Scorsese was to film the event, intending it to be the greatest film ever made of a rock concert. Which many thought it was.

The Band was about to say goodbye to the rock 'n' roll life, the one night stands with women, drugs, exhaustion, the emptiness, the loneliness and even despair, some or all of which had already claimed the lives of so many other musicians. It was not a route that Joni wished to venture down, she still needed her lucidity, still had so many other avenues to explore.

Bob Dylan and Joni were sitting together on the Queen Mary one day when Dylan asked, "if you were going to paint this room, what would you paint?" Joni replied "Well let me think. I'd paint the mirrored ball spinning. I'd paint the women in the

washroom, the band... later, all the stuff came back to me as part of a dream that became the song Paprika Plains".

Joni was renting a Manhattan apartment as a refuge from her travels, gorging herself on foreign films and decorating her apartment, whilst spending time in California, where, she said, "I live like a princess... I'm looked after". The New York apartment was a contrast, where everything was laid out neatly in the kitchen, a place that she could fill with the shopping she did herself and the plants she bought herself. It was important to her, this small domestic life, "because there definitely is something you lose in the trade". Like many others who found success, she fought against it overwhelming her. "If I had to live with less I can do it easily", she said before contradicting herself by saying that she was like the monkey with his hand stuck in the peanut jar; she had been seduced by the luxury, by the swimming pool. She found a way of dealing with it in her own mind at least, feeling that if she channelled her success into her music, tapped into it as a form of self-expression, she could finally enjoy the trappings of success.

New York also brought about involvement with another musician; Don Alias, an American jazz percussionist. Joni met him in 1977, and they became lovers; he would bring his band up to rehearse in the apartment, too. Don would play on her album Don Juan's Reckless Daughter, and the fact that he had played with Miles Davis, her childhood hero, with whom she hoped to play herself one day, didn't harm the relationship either. And possessive, "insanely jealous" Don (Joni could always hone in on them when life was too smooth) did as she had hoped and introduced her to the great man. Except that at the time, Miles Davis was taking any drugs that he could find having left the music business for a few years with bitterness as his motivation. Unfortunately, the meeting didn't go as planned, and Miles, high as a kite, made a pass for her before passing out. Collaboration was not to be it seemed.

She had barely played the piano since the cancelled tour in 1976,

but now, recovering from abscessed ovaries that had seen her in and out of hospital, she sat down at the piano and improvised chords. What emerged was something that excited her so much that she telephoned Henry Lewy, insisting that they go into the studio to record, because, as she told him, "I can't hit a wrong chord".

So even though Henry was not well either, into the studio they went, where Joni improvised with chords and produced some two hours of music. She later wrote the lyrics to Paprika Plains - discarding seventy lines before deciding on the final format - inspired by a cocaine dream that had come to her during the Rolling Thunder Tour. In Paprika Plains, Joni romped back to her childhood to tell of the conflict between those who had "traded their beads for bottles", and creativity. The song lasted for over sixteen minutes in length, with orchestral arrangements by Barclee School of Music Professor Michael Gibbs. He loved her "rough playing" and was inspired to talk to the singer in the poetic ideas that she loved. The two hit it off, Joni content to allow Michael his own creative freedom. They were surrounded with some of the best musicians in jazz such as Ron Carter and Harry Loofofsky, and the thought of improvisation with these made even Joni Mitchell nervous.

Paprika Plains found its way onto her new album, Don Juan's Reckless Daughter, on which she used not only Jaco Pastorius but another musician who was one of her top favourites, saxophonist Wayne Shorter. Shorter was part of the jazz fusion band Weather Report (Jaco Pastorius joined in 1976), and he appealed to Joni as a visionary, another man with a poetic ear who could paint word pictures and melt them into music, a man with an instinct for the right note or the right silence at the right moment.

Joni was close to the conclusion of her contract with Asylum Records when she made Don Juan and had given herself the freedom to be "looser" than she had ever been before. For the most part, the album is experimental jazz fusion, and although it garnered mixed reviews it did work its way up to number 25 on the Billboard charts. Whilst none of the singles broke into the top

MAIN IMAGE:
During The Last Waltz at Winterland on
November 25, 1976 in San Francisco, California

40, it still achieved gold status. Joni was unerring in her goals and sincerity, commercially acceptable or not, and her fans were still prepared to make the journey with her.

Joni wasn't going to help herself or the album when she dressed up as a pimp with a blackface for the cover photo. He was her "reputed alter ego", a black hipster called Art Nouveau or Claude. In the end, though, no one seemed to know it was her; Rolling Stone did and criticised her for implying that black people and third world countries knew how to enjoy themselves more, were possessed of more rhythm and mischievousness and that she was thus associating herself with them and disassociating herself from everyone else.

The magazine went on to say that she had gambled and lost after years of being exciting and unpredictable. "Mitchell's pretensions" it went on, "have shaped her appraisal of her own gifts", before turning the screw even harder by saying that she had not been a particularly original observer and never an "interesting chronicler" about anything other than her own experiences. In an article full of damning barbs, the double album was dismissed as "sapped of emotion and full of ideas that should have remained whims, melodies that should have been riffs, songs that should have been fragments... Joni Mitchell's talents stretched here to breaking point".

Not everyone thought so, and Joni's most free and most daring album with its famous song Dreamland – reflecting her visit to the carnival in Rio de Janeiro and filled with surrealist descriptions contrasting western society, it's hypocrisy and capitalist coldness with third world countries – Paprika Plains, Jericho, the rather uninterestingly conventional Off Night Backstreet, and with the Silky Veils of Ardor providing a dreamy conclusion, found its way onto the streets in December 1977.

When she was in her early teenage years, Joni's jazz icon had been Miles Davis. Now she was about to embark on one of the most exciting projects of her career with a man who had become one of the most legendary bandleaders and players in the history of jazz; Joni attributed its birth to a magical series of "amazing coincidences".

Charlie Mingus had played with the greatest jazz musicians of the age and boasted an even fiercer reputation than Joni's (who needed "purity of spirit") for demanding emotional truth from his music and his musicians, demands often backed up with physical violence that belied his ability to pen love songs of enormous tenderness. His many marriages indicated that his love was as hamstrung by his unfulfilled and torn expectation as Joni's.

Joni discovered a like-minded musical soul, a man who could not sit on a musical line for long without taking it to new and unexpected, unexplored lands, pouring his whirling emotions, searching and longings into music that soared, roared, confronted and caressed. He drew from music anywhere that inspired him, fusing Dixieland with classical and mixing in behop or the church, flamenco and verbal sauntering if that's what his inspiration encountered. The men he used could exist without the crowded air of harmony, men like brilliant pianist Don Pullen and reeds virtuoso Eric Dolphy, players willing to enter the carefully structured Mingus chaos and return refreshed. Again, Joni saw a kindred spirit in the way Mingus hugged his experiences to his inner self and wrought his compositions from his soul whatever the cost; his explosive temperament often tested and broke the loyalty of his musicians, and it marbled his music as he wrestled and cajoled it to express the Mingus truth.

When Mingus and Mitchell met, Mingus was already in the wheelchair to which his incurable progressive degenerative illness, Lou Gehrig's' disease – ALS, amyotrophic lateral sclerosis – had condemned him and which would finally take him from the world in January 1979 aged just 56, whilst he was still working with Joni.

Charlie Mingus was a deeply religious man, and as he pondered

the music he would never write, the friends he would never see
again, his death sentence made him want to engage with the
man who mattered most to him; God; Charlie's wife, Sue, was
helping in the search to find a suitable method for Charlie to
make it happen.

"I want to speak to you about God" said Charlie to Producer
Daniele Senatore one day, who understandably felt himself to
be slightly overwhelmed by the request. So he directed Charlie's
thoughts towards T. S. Eliot's Four Quartets in which Eliot
attempted to "Expose the reader to the ideas of religion". Charlie
read and discussed the poems with his wife. Here was fire, here
was fierceness, here was something that he wanted to set to
music as a fitting epitaph, here was the key to music that he had
been searching for, for a long time.

Senatore had heard Joni's Reckless Daughter, and Sue and he
listened to the record. They were both sure that this women could
be the key to unlocking Charlie's last musical gift to the world;
even though Charlie had not really known the Canadian's work,
her musical curiosity chimed with Charlie's; two intrepid explorers.

They made contact with her.

Joni never felt that Charlie fully understood what he was reading
and thought it inappropriate material for a man in the last months
of his life, devoid of relevance to his situation. Neither did she like
the Four Quartets, or even poetry in general, considering the vast
majority of it pretentious. Charlie, on the other hand loved poetry,
had written his own and set other poets to music, also enlisting
Alan Ginsberg to officiate at his wedding to Sue.

Neither did Joni know much more about Charlie Mingus than his
name. Which might have made her an inappropriate collaborator;
which is what John Guerin thought whilst persuading her that such
a chance would have been manna from heaven for every other
musician. But perhaps it was the call by David Geffen not to do it for

RIGHT:
**Joni Mitchell and Pat Metheny perform during
the Berkeley Jazz Festival at the Greek Theatre
in May 1979 in Berkeley, California**

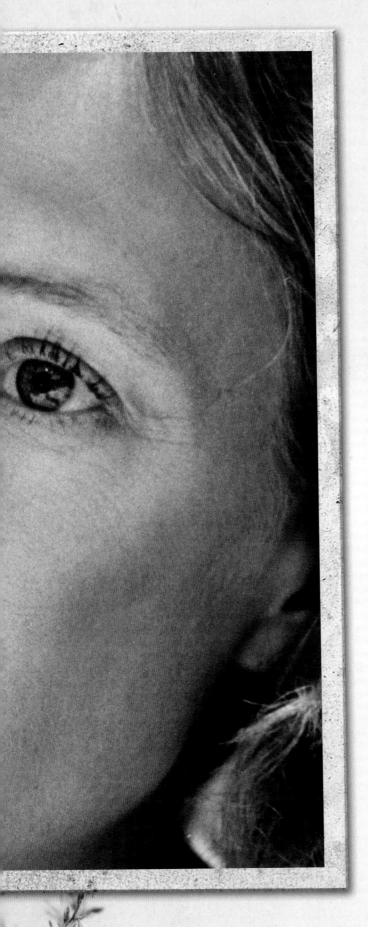

fear of alienating her fans that persuaded her to do the opposite. Whatever the reason, and despite her reservations, she went ahead.

And she was filled with admiration from the moment they met in his apartment on the 44th floor facing the Hudson River in New York, admiration that slid into adoration for "this beautiful face, full of the devil and beautiful light... a man who was capable of expressing many emotions". Adoration that made her slip from her own high standards above cliché to ask him one day "how are you?" To which he laconically replied, "Oh, I'm dying". Joni read the poems and then declined Charlie's offer. But when he rang back to say that he had composed seven pieces – he named them Joni I through to Joni VII – singing into a tape recorder, to which Sy Johnson then added the strange chords, she went to see him. When he played out the melodies, she found them somehow old-fashioned; "it didn't seem fresh to me" was her first thought. But by then, she was already caught in his magic web and her defences collapsed. She even spent ten days with him in Mexico City, where he went to visit a faith healer, "A beautiful radiant visit".

She would have just a few weeks to complete her work. Her task was to use this music to inform her lyrics and at the same time do justice to a genius saying goodbye to life. (He also asked her to write the words to two pieces that he had written in 1959 for the Mingus Ah Um album. One of these was Self-Portrait in Three Colours, a project that must have appealed strongly to her painterly soul, but one that would ultimately not be concluded.) It was a mammoth task for a woman who could not read music and would, therefore, need to memorise everything, expressing the final emotions of a musical titan, his voice when his own was failing. Never before had she written words for someone else's music. It was an incredible act of faith by the bassist to entrust this extraordinary, magical time to "that skinny-ass folksinger".

And the enormity of the task, music using a wider range than she had ever worked with before, the realisation that she had misjudged the complex nature of Charlie's music, blocked her at

LEFT:
Joni Mitchell portrait, 1980

MAIN IMAGE:
(L to R) Klaus Voormann,
John Mayall, Joni Mitchell,
photographer/editor Debby
Chesher and Commander Cody
during the promotion for the
'Starart' book that included
art works by them and other
musicians at the Gramercy
Park Hotel in New York City on
December 12, 1979

first, rendering her unable to write – but did not prevent her from painting, which she did for a fortnight, waiting for inspiration; a great deal of the art for the album cover arose during those weeks. The self-doubt persisted as she worked on the songs, often convinced that she could not pull it off, but determined to submerge herself in the jazz she had been toying with on the periphery. And she felt an affinity with this man who had been stamped with the adjective "difficult", as she had been, also. She wandered Manhattan in search of the entrance door to the project.

Working for someone else, Joni was at the receiving end of what she would usually ladle out to others; Mingus was hard to satisfy, and she would feel the lash of his verbal whip if she missed his notes; a demanding, scolding master. She was unaccustomed to scolding and demanding, unaccustomed to submittance; something that ultimately, on Goodbye Pork Pie Hat, for example, she found herself unable to do. She could not subsume herself in someone else's dream, she had to remain true to herself. Although she tried to weave the Charlie Mingus she had come to know into the words, he would only ever be the colour scheme and not the heart of what she wrote for him. The intense chocolate consistency of a Charlie Mingus session would relegate her words, and she did not like her words to be relegated, even in this situation.

Joni would have to finish the album without Charlie, who died in January 1979. She did so with musicians she felt comfortable with, members of the Weather Report, Herbie Hancock, Wayne Shorter, to produce a sound that would not have been to Charlie's liking. It became Joni's record instead, the brilliance of the brilliant jazz musicians diluted in favour of the voice.

Joni loved working with her musicians, however, the alchemists, as she called them, this circle of magicians were just as exciting as "watching two birds disappear up a guy's sleeve".

And Henry Lewy praised Jaco Pistorius in the highest terms saying

MAIN IMAGE:
Joni Mitchell and B.B. King, 1980

that he played the bass as though he were playing an orchestra, and this affected Joni's own musical activity; she began using her voice and guitar in ways she had never done before.

Two of the songs were Joni's entirely; "God must be a Boogie Man" and "The Wolf That Lives in Lindsey". Joni based them on the words of chapter one of Charlie's Beneath the Underdog, his memoir. Other titles are more direct references to Charlie's life; A Chair in the Sky is an obvious one; "But now Manhattan holds me to a chair in the sky ... there's things I wish I'd done, some friends I'm going to miss, beautiful lovers, I never got the chance to kiss", and The Dry Cleaner from Des Moines referencing Charlie's luck on the one-armed bandits; "I'm stalking the slot that's hot, I keep hearing bells all around me, jingling the lucky jackpot, they keep you tantalised, they keep you reaching for your wallet, here in fool's paradise". It was a song that appealed greatly to Charlie Mingus. In God must be a Boogie Man, the song she wrote after Charlie Mingus's death, but which she called a "condensation of the first four chapters of his book", she takes the idea that he talked about in his memoir, his trilogy of characteristics, the three aspects of himself, strong, detached, open, and uses it to create

the song; "He is three, one is in the middle, unmoved, waiting... which one do you think he'd want the world to see, well, world opinion is not a lot of help, when a man's only trying to find out how to feel about himself!"

The album was released on the 13th of June 1979, eventually peaking at number 17.

David Geffen's prediction that radio stations would abandon her proved all too correct. The general consensus seemed to be that the songs were too extenuated and too sluggish to achieve any great impact, ponderous, in contrast to the light-hearted Charlie Mingus of reality, the six-and-a-half minutes of The Wolf That Lives in Lindsey cited as a chief offender. Individual highlights were praised, but the improvisational freedom Charlie enjoyed with abandon was missing on this 'memorial' album. Reviewers acknowledged the growth in the singer's vocal powers but criticised that she had become too cute with lyrics.

MAIN IMAGE:
Joni Mitchell plays acoustic guitar as she performs on stage at Studio 54, New York, New York, April 2, 1982

FROM LOVE TO VIOLENCE
AND BACK AGAIN

Mingus, the man and the album, seemed to kick some stones loose in Joni, for she suddenly embarked on a series of interviews, ending her eight-year self-imposed moratorium on sitting down with Rolling Stone, which had been her way of punishing them for a searing article in 1971 which had dubbed her "Old lady of the year".

Not only that, she had not toured since running off the stage three years previously, but now she set out on a full-scale sweep of the United States. It began in July 1979, just a few months after Mingus had passed away. L. A. Express rejected the offer to be her backing band, so with Jaco Pastorius as a musical director, she put a new band together consisting of Michael Brecker on saxophone, Jaco Pastorius on bass, Pat Metheny on guitar, Don alias on percussion and Lyle Mays on keyboards. The warm up act, and providing backing vocals, were the Persuasions. She wasn't always entirely happy with the choices of musician and would have preferred Wayne Shorter on sax. Perhaps the difference was academic, as Joni never allowed the music to even be on a par with the attention her words should get, let alone upstage them with virtuosic solos.

"Jazzers" weren't word people, she commented in an interview, they were note people and she instructed them to follow the words, to get in between the words. "You can't dominate them. You've got to support them and in the breaks where there are no words - Bam! - there's a kind of free for all. Everybody is playing off of everybody else."

Jaco and the other musicians were not given much breathing space, and because of his adherence to Hejira, not even the songs from the Mingus album, which were ostensibly why the tour had been put together in the first place, got much airplay. In fact, though no one but Joni might have known it, her ten-year foray into experimentation would be coming to a close with this tour. She had reacted to the thought of returning to rock 'n' roll like a vampire to garlic, yet as she approached the changing musical world of the 80s, she chased after the very thing she had despised, no longer the leader but the follower, a diluted version of herself and those who were the big names of the 80s.

The Mingus tour moved across America, concluding with a concert at the Santa Barbara County Bowl, which was recorded and filmed. The editing of these tapes into what would become her next album, Shadows and Light, would occupy her for the whole of the following year and be her final release for Asylum Records. Jaco, the man who had dominated the jazz world and mastered his instrument and many musical genres like no other, would be acclaimed for his performance at Santa Barbara, delivering music of unparalleled excellence.

For Jaco, the 1980s would see him diagnosed with bipolar disease and drugs and alcohol dominate his life more and more as he continued on a downward spiral.

For Joni, there was also trouble ahead, though not quite so dramatic in nature.

Whilst she had been working on her new album, David Geffen had started his own record company in 1980 having sold Asylum. Geffen persuaded Joni to sign with him, seducing her with the

offer of a large advance. She was, after all, as susceptible to money and fame as anyone else. She received some of the advance but not the rest; Geffen had not told her that he would retain her income until he had paid off the $225,000 it had cost him to buy out her contract with Elektra. Many years later she would complain that she had never seen a royalty cheque from him.

Shadows and Light got no further than number 38 on the Billboard charts when it was released in September 1980, and the single Why Do Fools Fall in Love? didn't even make the hot 100.

Inducted into the Canadian Hall of Fame in 1981, her private life continued to have complications for Joni. Don Alias and she were still together and had even considered marriage and children. But the irrationally jealous Alias found it hard to cope with Joni's open relationship with her ex-boyfriends, and on at least two occasions he beat her up. On the second occasion, the cause was a dinner with John Guerin, who she still hired as a musician; a dinner that went on until the early hours of the morning. When she got home, Alias attacked her.

And it was John, his instincts honed by his long association with Joni, who had a premonition that something was wrong with her. He abandoned his studio session, went to her house and heard her moaning as he approached. He hesitated, thinking she might be with her lover, but then changed his mind and went in to find her black and blue from the beating. With his deep and passionate love of women and his deep feelings for Joni still, he was probably the best person to have been at her side.

Despite these traumas, and being put into victim mode, she still did not abandon the relationship. Not until Alias tried one more time to hit her did she finally get the message and stopped the relationship with the words "you can't control yourself and I can't stay here".

Another failed relationship to feed the lyrical accompaniment to life,

MAIN IMAGE:
Joni Mitchell and Herbie Hancock perform live at The Greek Theatre in 1981 in Berkeley, California

had left the way open to wander into love's lair again; the next man she met there would also be a musician. The relationship seemed to be a metaphor of what would happen to Joni in the Michael Jackson wonderland of the 1980s as her career and musical judgment splintered and the vagaries of the industry turned and bit her with the help of tax laws.

Joni had said that if she had a goal at all, it was to make modern American music. That should have been a red light for anyone listening.

She stepped back from Mingus and began work on a new album for 1982, Wild Things Run Fast, by which time she had already moved back towards pop, infused now with the snazzy beats of the 80s.

Wild Things Run Fast, she said, drew inspiration from the Police and Talking Heads; she had heard them during a Caribbean trip in 1981, and it was the drumbeats that turned her towards making a more rhythmic album, as she described it.

After all the shenanigans with Alias, John Guerin would join his last session for his erstwhile lover with this album, which featured a bored-looking Joni on the cover leaning on a television showing a picture of, yes, wild horses – running through water. And then she explains why, in Chinese Café; "Caught in the middle Carol, we're middle-class... we're middle aged, we were wild in the old days".

Time may be passing in the songs, and Joni wistfully speaks of uranium money "booming in the old home town now, tearing the old landmarks down now, paving over brave little parks", but love was always the fulcrum of Joni Mitchell's songwriting, and just to make clear how important it was, the word is mentioned 57 times on the album.

And it's love that's on her mind in real life, too, because as Jaco became more unreliable, a new bass player was hired to take his

place – onstage and in bed; Larry Klein. Joni thought that she had finally found the genuine article, because soon after the album was released in October 1982, she and Larry married in a Buddhist ceremony. It was November the 21st 1982. Larry was 13 years her junior, but they were soon inseparable to the extent that Joni even named him co-producer for her next albums, reversing a lifelong habit of insisting on being her own producer. The marriage would last for 12 years.

Joni knew that she needed a new way forward and hoped for help from the younger man. The 'help' stretched out over the next 15 years, and for Larry Klein, it was the start of an extraordinary learning experience with someone who he considered to be like no one else on the planet. They were two peas in a pod, discussing anything and everything, and to Klein, it must have seemed as though their lives would go on forever, so intimate was their union; he was smitten with this funny, talented, clever and stimulating woman. But his partner was Joni Mitchell; love was a thing to be dissected after it had fled its romantic provenance. And flee it would, unable to withstand her narcissism and the seemingly bottomless well of her anger, as he reported. Nothing lasts for long, she would intone on her album. Expecting the worst wasn't a good basis for a relationship.

Nonetheless, she even enlisted the help of the Bible for the track named Love, taking the words from 1 Corinthians 13, when St Paul addresses the Corinthians; "If I speak in the tongues of men or of angels, but do not have love, I am only a resounding gong or a clanging cymbal". Discarding all the archaic Bible speak, she distilled the essence of the text in this paean to love; "Love never looks for love, love is not puffed up, or envious, or touchy, because it rejoices in the truth not in iniquity", before going on to say that love is the greatest of the trinity of faith, hope and love, repeating the word three times as the song ends.

Perhaps it was this cascade of love fulfilled and not the barbed-wire enclosure of a relationship that Joni normally described that disappointed those used to her poetic shark attacks. It was also

RIGHT:
Joni Mitchell pictured backstage wearing a trilby style hat prior to her concert at Wembley Arena, London on 23rd April 1983

devoid of most of the convex and concave lyrics that had been their predecessors and so thrilled listeners. The pop-rock-jazz album also suffered from Joni's attempt to modernise, maybe to chase the elusive hit to maintain the high-maintenance lifestyle that she had become accustomed to.

It might seem extraordinary then, that she chose this period when she seemed to be jumping on the bandwagon of commercial acceptance – this form of music that seemed alien to everything that she had held up to be valuable – to reveal the greatest secret of her life.

Perhaps she thought, finally yielding to her need for public confession, that she could hide the secret, Kelly, in full view in easy listening, soothing vibes and piano music. "My child's a stranger, I bore her, but I could not raise her". The words come in the first verse of Chinese Café, when she is remembering how life used to be and reflecting on what it has turned into, what she and Carol have turned into, i.e., their mothers at the same age. Time goes, and that life, that Joni, have all gone, but her need for love remains.

On an album devoted to love, the reference to Kelly has of course found a perfect home

Once she had poured out the love on the album, "Yes, I do – I love you, I really love you, yes I do – yes I do, I love you!" is the repeated mantra on Underneath the Street Light, swearing on everything she sets eyes on that she truly does, Joni took the songs out on tour. It was to be her final tour as a solo artist and also the longest that she would ever do; armed with an electric guitar, it also proved to be her most physically strenuous.

The musicians behind her now, were Larry Klein on bass, Michael Landau on guitar – who broke with the traditions of his predecessors in her bands, forcing a new hard-rock sound into her songs and of whom Joni was critical because of his "sense of musical architecture" according to Klein – Vinnie Colaiuta on drums and Russell Ferranti on keyboards. Joni would play guitar, dulcimer and piano.

"Love", Joni mused in an interview; "It's a funny word to use. It's like love means different things to different people. It's like God". Then she went on to say that indifference was probably the antithesis of love. "I mean, that's probably the worst. Not hate. Hate and love are not that different".

They set off on the 28th of February 1983 for Japan with Klein as

musical director. By the time they had played their final concert in the Red Rock Centre Theatre in Morrison, CO., they had passed through Australia and New Zealand, the United Kingdom and Ireland and eight other European countries. Klein remembered that the tour was idyllic with all the musicians enjoying making music with each other, revelling in each other's company both on and off the stage whether working in a concert or at a party post concert. Drugs seemed to help rather than hinder in making this a smooth experience in which band members and the crew were not separated by status; everyone was a friend and Klein would smooth out any musical inconsistencies along the way leaving Joni free from any possible resentments from the musicians.

But touring took its toll of the singer, who was still smoking heavily, a habit that was finally beginning to have an adverse effect on her vocal cords. The song A Case of You, for example, had to be transposed to a lower key to accommodate her changing range. Coffee would not help her difficulties in sleeping, and her 24-hour waking/sleeping patterns would not synchronise with sound checks and flight schedules.

And when it was all over, the financial rewards were meagre for her, once band, crew, arenas, managers and producers had all taken their share. Joni's dislike of dealing with those aspects of her life cost her dear. And yet when she did realise what the consequences

of her lack of attention to finances meant for her, after the Refuge world tour, Klein noticed that she began to change and a process of embitterment set in "that resulted in her becoming angry more and more of the time". She fell into a permanent and destructive search for those who were causing her this distress. As though this were not enough stress, she was hit by a tax bill in California and her housekeeper accused the singer of abusing her.

Klein felt that those accusations were not entirely unjust if perhaps exaggerated. Her housekeeper walked away with $250,000, in an agreement not designed to make Joni sleep more soundly.

She had attempted to mould herself to fit into the new decade, and the distortion of her inner compass, her deepening sense of being at the receiving end of life, was causing intense anger. This was not a forest in which it was wise to dwell for long. But Joni had gone into fighting mode against the "shallow, stupid people, keeping the economy going by being these frightened consumers. America works on that fear: it's in, it's out."

SIZZLE AND FRY MUSIC

With Wild Things Run Fast languishing on the number 25 spot, Joni tried to keep at bay the wolves of worry about her personal situation, obvious anger at the far-right conservative world growing around her and the hypocrisy of organised religion, plus her tiredness, by occupying herself writing new songs.

As 1984 came around, Elliot Roberts and David Geffen suggested bringing in an outside producer with experience in the kind of music they were aiming to create – which Joni hated, calling it "sizzle and fry" music. Thomas Dolby was brought in, a British synthpop producer and performer, who Geffen hoped would be able to synthesise Joni Mitchell with the era in which she felt musically stranded; Wild Things Run Fast had proven that her lyrics were not comfortable bedfellows with the new synthetic music.

Thomas Dolby had admired Joni ever since he'd bought the album Blue. He was a synth wizard, and Joni wanted to get her critical analysis of the times across on the wave of the best technological sounds available; hit the era with its own methods. In the end, Joni Mitchell just could not be welded onto the 1980s. But try she had to.

The new album was, appropriately, to be called Dog Eat Dog, and the studio work through 1985, she hoped would be a welcome retreat from the gnawing world. She employed a whole raft of musicians that included Wayne Shorter, Michael Landau and Vinnie Colaiuta, and also Larry Klein, Thomas Dolby and even the spoken vocals of Rob Steiger, on the track Tax Free.

Yet the experience turned out to be anything but restful.

Klein metamorphosed from a player into a producer, which

wasn't to Joni's liking at all, and she didn't pull her punches describing him in later years. She accused him of being a "puffed-up dwarf", tyrannical and insecure, who used divide and conquer tactics to wreck all of her relationships. She felt that he was jealous of her relationship with Henry Lewy, with whom years of co-working had produced a wavelength of understanding peculiar to themselves.

It became the most expensive album of her career, chiefly because she insisted on sitting in with Thomas Dolby, and of course, altering, experimenting and discarding work that Thomas had already done. Her style of piano playing did not gel well with the complexity of Thomas's sound designs, and he found the impulsive dismissal of his work painful at the time. He did not realise that, despite having asked for him to be in the studio, she was not happy for him to be there, so her music business stories of Greece, Miles Davis and all points in between, the fact that she lent him her Mercedes convertible, endeared the singer to him. Her true feelings only came out many years later; "slimy little bugger". Their relationship deteriorated to such a level that she finally told him, "If we need you, we'll call you". Matters were not helped when Dolby apparently claimed ownership of the song Lucky Girl for which he had written music but that only Wayne Shorter had been able to rescue from chaos.

Perhaps the most fraught low point was when she ended up in a screaming telephone call with Dolby and his manager. So much for the rest she needed. All of this meant that it became the most unpleasant recording session she'd ever had. So incensed was she by the whole experience that she fired Elliot. And got Peter Asher, Jane Asher's brother, instead – which led to fights with him, a man that Joni says she never trusted. But as both of them were taking cocaine, according to Asher, it's hardly surprising that Joni saw herself as a Canadian version of Don Quixote. The arguments were destined to continue long after the album was released and even further into the future, with Peter Asher

---

MAIN IMAGE:
Joni Mitchell portrait, 1988

rejecting Joni's implication that because he had James Taylor as a client, he would not wish her the "utmost success". Joni was a genius, and he had tried his best for her album, he said.

Dog Eat Dog, the title that seemed to describe the atmosphere in the studio, was marbled through with Joni's anger, and the lyrics kicked out at her targets; TV evangelists, politicians, lawyers, materialism. The track Fiction took aim at popular cultural materialism, and The Three Great Stimulants, considered by some as the worst song that she ever made, became self-righteous and preachy, but was balanced out by Tax Free, which used vocals from Rob Steiger to take tele-evangelists to task.

The album was released in October 1985 to a less than enthusiastic welcome and dragged itself as far as number 63 in the US charts.

However ruthless she might be in the studio towards her work, she seemed incapable of defending herself against the dominance of her partners. Years later, she would remember that when she became pregnant in that year of 1985, Klein "dragged" her off on a European holiday. The memories were open wounds; Klein gave no thought to his pregnant wife, never thought to bring her to a doctor; those were her memories.

She still smoked like a trooper, though, and on January the 28th 1986, she lost the baby. There were no comforting words, he did not hold her in his arms, she remembered, and then he left her to go to England.

Klein admitted later that he had no idea what effect a miscarriage could have on a person, didn't realise how serious it was either physically or psychologically. He had had to leave what he remembered as being a press tour in Europe, not a holiday, for his job as a producer in England, and Joni had told him he could go. Joni, he said, would never take care of herself and did not like others telling her she should, the implication being that it was not unsurprising that something should happen. This love had

certainly turned to more than mere indifference and there was no way back for the marriage.

In 1986, Amnesty International staged a televised concert during the A Conspiracy of Hope Tour of six benefit concerts. At the Giants Stadium in New Jersey in Rutherford New Jersey on Sunday the 15th of June 1986, Joni Mitchell replaced Pete Townshend and slipped out onto the stage between Bryan Adams and U2. It was a brave thing to do. Quietly strumming a song from Dog Eat Dog, she sang her angry message of human complacency and weakness; it was impossible to hear her over the noise from the audience. Looking back, she mustered a sense of humour when a shattered water glass came flying her way. The audience had been hurling things all afternoon. "Quit pitching shit up here" she said into the microphone, but she may just as well have been whistling into the wind; she often felt that she was anyway.

But as she walked the streets of New York, she met the people who felt connected to her music, and they couldn't do enough for her to make her still feel that she was wanted and loved. Even if she did berate them in her songs.

Joni, at that time, was in the recording studio preparing songs for her 13th studio album, which she had called Chalk Mark in a Rain Storm. She recorded in a variety of studios, from Peter Gabriel's Ashcombe House in Bath in England, where, for a while she and Gabriel struck up a friendship and recorded a duet, My Secret Place, about "the uniting spirit of two people at the beginning of a relationship" according to Joni. The relationship did not last long, a souring that Klein attributed to too many conversations in which she pushed her "didactically nihilistic view of the world".

Klein had written three pieces that Joni wanted for the album, eventually turning them into Lakota, Snakes and Ladders and The Tea Prophecy.

Whatever her views about musicians, among others, selling out, she brought musical stars into the studio for her own album, in

the attempt to bring it into line with their successes. Thus, not only Peter Gabriel can be heard, but Don Henley, Billy Idol, Tom Petty, Benjamin Orr from the Cars and Willie Nelson. Joni had brought in a proper drummer this time, Manu Katché, who had worked with Peter Gabriel, and he can be heard throughout the album, a great relief to fans who had fretted about the synthesisers – which Joni had not yet finished with, however.

The songs roamed between the love of My Secret Place to the agonies of war in The Beat of Black Wings (about a Vietnam vet struggling with the psychological aftermath of the war) taking in the destruction of Native American culture in Lakota, and water pollution in Cool Water along the way.

Before the album was released in March 1988, she made another of her rare TV appearances, on Showtime Coast to Coast hosted by Herbie Hancock. The idea was to explore the jazz possibilities in two songs from her Hejira album, and Joni's voice was superb, despite, or maybe because, of the huskiness that had set in; the smoking would soon transform her voice from soprano to alto. Returned to a jazz setting devoid of 1980s electronics, it was a chance to see what might have been if she had not executed a deft pirouette after Mingus.

Most reviews of the album were favourable; Rolling Stone gave it three stars praising her clean and concise wordplay but criticising the melodic inaccessibility, the lack of strongly constructed melody lines. The magazine was, finally, dismissive, ending its critique with the words, "this album doesn't invite repeated listenings; in that sense, Chalk Mark in a Rain Storm is all too aptly named, for its pleasures simply wash away with time".

With its world music leanings, Chalk Mark in a Rain Storm made it to number 45 in America.

There has always existed a tendency to believe that the stars of the world are possessed of fuller and more rounded character attributes than the mere mortals listening to their music. Joni had been disabused of that idea long before, and she had her opinion of the "childish competitiveness and lack of professionalism" amongst many of them reaffirmed when she played in Berlin on Pink Floyd's The Wall. Her trailer park experiences with artists had been very bad in the past, but she was prepared to try again. She attempted to talk to many of them, with no success, coming to the conclusion that there wasn't a single adult in the entire pack, finding all of the responses to her attempts to communicate "very strange".

But at least the 1980s were over, the experimentation with a genre that suited her like an iron mask relegated to history. She was about to feel renewed, to Come in From the Cold.

MAIN IMAGE:

Joni Mitchell performing at Farm Aid in Champaigne, Illinois on September 22, 1985

MAIN IMAGE:
Joni Mitchell portrait, 1988

A MEETING WITH THE PAST

J oni spent much of 1990 recording the songs for her next album Night Ride Home. She abandoned thoughts of using guest musicians, using instead her core of trusted companions; Wayne Shorter, Michael Landau, Larry Klein and Vinnie Colaiuta. Overflowing with loneliness - one offshoot of the lack of acknowledgement that she felt she had received from the music industry - the result was an album of greater intimacy and accessibility than she had produced for some time. It was an album about being an adult dealing with the problems of midlife, taking in adolescence - the song Cherokee Louise picking up the hot coal of child abuse, and then Ray's Dad's Cadillac - and passing through the end of the world - Slouching Toward Bethlehem, based on the W. B. Yeats' poem The Second Coming - just in case listeners thought she was no longer interested in that. And love, of course, gets a nostalgic role in the final track Two Grey Rooms. As a "crazy, elusive, gorgeous" vintage Joni Mitchell song, it relates the story of someone who has, apparently, rented a flat to watch the man "loved 30 years ago" walk past his window. The inspiration for the story of obsession, Joni's word, is a German aristocrat, part of the circle around German film director and enfant terrible Rainer Werner Fassbinder - another artist with whom Joni felt an association - unable mentally to let go of his youthful lover, renting two grey rooms so that he can watch his former flame on his way to and from work. The element of self-destructive behaviour must have chimed deeply with Joni.

The title song Night Ride Home was about as pretty as she had produced for two decades, almost an immediate statement that the 1980s Joni had been consigned to the dustbin. No leaping vocals forcing the melody into strange territory, this was a symbolic musical night ride home for Joni, too, in love "with the man beside me, we love the open road".

Many considered this album to be the point at which Joni settled into accepting that she was no longer the iconoclastic leader of an age; this was the last of her great creative projects.
It was also the last of four that Joni would produce for David Geffen. "For one reason or another, they were viewed as being out of sync with the '80s. But I was out of sync with the '80s. Thank God! To be in sync with these times, in my opinion, was to be degenerating both morally and artistically. Materialism became a virtue; greed was hip."

The rather kitschy video for the track Night Ride Home probably didn't help that the album, released in February 1991, only managed to ride up to number 41 in the American charts; nor did it produce any hit singles.

The love that she had thought might last, finally disintegrated. Larry Klein and Joni filed for divorce. Klein had experienced a rollercoaster of artistic and personal growth with a woman like no other. Being Joni's partner had proven to be an enormous strain once anger and bitterness had been introduced to dilute the affection. Depression had also taken its toll, but he had wanted to stay with her, hoping for a change in direction. It was not to be, and his hopes were dashed with Joni's response; "I'm not going to be changing much at this point".

Which might have been a response to asking about her musical direction, too, where she had reintroduced acoustic guitars and piano, and as if in confirmation that everyone else had been waiting for this moment, they encouraged her by awarding her next album a Grammy.

In keeping with the singer's penchant for literary themes and associating herself with her subject matter on her album covers, Turbulent Indigo sports Joni painted in an impressionist style with her ear bandaged à la Vincent van Gogh. Joni decided to use the

MAIN IMAGE:
Joni Mitchell performs on stage at The Wall Concert, Berlin, 21st July 1990

MAIN IMAGE:
Joni Mitchell with Roger Waters at a soundcheck prior to his
performance in Water's The Wall concert in Berlin, Germany
on 21st July 1990

image after years of frustration about what she considered to be the lack of recognition in the public voice for the growth that had taken place along her musical trajectory, something, she felt, that had also affected her record label. "What do I have to do? Cut my ear off?" she asked herself.

Turbulent Indigo leads us through global warming, AIDS, the women consigned to the Roman Catholic church's Magdalen Asylums in Ireland, their workhouses for 'fallen women', and consumerism. The Magdalen Laundries struck more than a discord in Joni, who was herself an unmarried mother. "These bloodless brides of Jesus, if they just once glimpsed their groom, then they would know, and they'd drop the stones concealed behind their rosaries".

And love? The track Not to Blame, portrays the love that Joni had held high in so many other songs now producing agony; "Six hundred thousand doctors are putting on rubber gloves and they're poking at the miseries made of love".

Joni's former lover Jackson Browne had been accused by Daryl Hannah, his then girlfriend, of hospitalising her after a beating in 1992. Joni never confirmed or denied that this song referred to her former lover, including him, however, by universalising the song's theme. It was one of Joni's character hiccups that she was drawn to idolise men like Picasso and Miles Davis; "Most of my heroes are monsters, unfortunately, and they are men".

Rolling Stone considered this album poetic, highly musical but very, very sad; Mitchell's best album since the mid-1970s and her artistry undiminished. The sound was described as spare, the songs anchored by Mitchell's piano, although they considered that "it's on guitar... that Mitchell is a true stylist".

Released in October 1994, the album reached number 47 on the American charts. Hers was a harsh message, after all, and one of the harshest on the album, Sex Kills, she sang throughout America; TV presented her with a platform to do so.

In 1993, Joni's mother introduced her daughter to a man called Don Freed, a fellow Canadian, also a singer and songwriter, whose themes revolved mainly around the Canadian prairies.

He was in many ways, the ideal companion for Joni; he lived simply, without a car, and for many years even without a television. Freed moved to Los Angeles to be with his new girlfriend, and they "sat around a pool for six months". It became clear to him that that was something he could not continue to do. So they arranged their lives to make their relationship workable for each other and maintained separate living arrangements, visiting one another in between their many commitments.

The relationship with Don was a gleam of sunshine in a period when she had begun to feel that she and music had mutually lost interest in one another, despite the fact that in 1995 she was the Billboard Century Award winner, an award given annually "to an artist to acknowledge the uncommon excellence of a still unfolding body of work".

That year was significant in another way, too, that would rekindle her interest in music.

In May, she had met a young jazz drummer at the New Orleans Jazz festival, called Brian Blade. Blade was an exceptional drummer rhythmically and emotionally; his sensitivity was as feather light as his respect and his need for minimalism and musical space was powerful. His mastery of the drum kit was second to none, and perhaps more importantly, he was an admirer of Joni's music.

Joni's famed cynicism had, by now, been honed to scalpel sharpness; her search for purity of spirit had rendered her indifferent to almost all music that she heard. With Brian Blade, she knew she had found a kindred spirit. They played together on November the 5th at a dinner honouring Gary Trudeau the cartoonist.

One day later, they played together again; this time the singer was holding her new, green, electric guitar. A godsend on two counts: firstly, it was very light, a not inconsiderable improvement considering she had back problems, and secondly it enabled her to program all of her tunings. True, the sound was digital and not acoustic, but at least she was still playing. She had been inspired to play gigs with Brian, to be seen on television with him.

In 1996 – the year that Wayne Shorter's wife of 25 years died in a plane crash – Joni won two Grammys for Best Pop Album and best Album Packaging for Turbulent Indigo, as well as the Gemini Award in Canada and the Polar Music Prize in Sweden. She released a greatest hits album, which floundered around at number 161 in the US charts.

As she embarked on her latest album, her voice was not only assaulted by nicotine but now by ageing vocal cords, and the soprano range vanished for ever.

Re-enthused by Brian Blade, she and the drummer began making frequent trips to the studio. From their collaboration, emerged a new album; Taming the Tiger. There had been an expectation that she would never release another album with new material, especially as she had indicated that the New Orleans Jazz Festival was going to be her swan song.

By the time Taming the Tiger was taking shape in the studio, something momentous had occurred in the singer's life. Joni had been in contact with her daughter; Kilauren Gibb. Kilauren had contacted Joni's manager and left a message. Joni called back and left one of her own; "Hi, it's Joni. Please call me. I'm here. I'm overwhelmed".

They met in March 1997 in Los Angeles. It was to prove as volatile a relationship as any that Joni had with men, the similarities between mother and daughter destined to cause rifts.

The Taming the Tiger album whittled down the number of musicians again; this time only Landau, Klein and Shorter

remained of her core players, now joined by Brian Blade on drums. Joni's cover art showed a picture of her in a large-brimmed straw hat, immediately reminiscent of the early days of her career.

Released in September 1998, it eventually found a home on slot 75 of the American charts, with 133,000 sales.

Reviews were favourable, some considering the album one of her best in which she used her new guitar synthesiser for a jazzy sound that sometimes almost ranged into the orchestral. Critics noted the red threads stretching back to The Hissing of Summer Lawns and the Hejira albums; the sound was also sparse, shades of Hejira, and Wayne Shorter was singled out for his playing.

Joni had funnelled her contempt for the music business into the lyrics; "I'm a runaway from the record biz, from the hoods in the hood and the whiny white kids" she writes on the title track, a business in which "every song (is) just a one night stand", and with Don now a permanent fixture in life, it was no surprise that she came out with My Best to You, a song from one of the earliest western singing groups, Sons of the Pioneers.

Her love songs on this occasion are far from the happy ever after stable; one is a song of love lost, Man from Mars, without whom "There is no centre to my life", and the other, Love Puts on a New Face, takes a romantic occasion and splashes it with cynicism, so that when the lover says he wishes she were there with him, she replies "send me some pictures then, and I'll paint pyrotechnic explosions of your autumn till we meet again", before confessing that she misses his touch and embrace, but expressing her doubts about her feelings because "Love puts on a new face... Love has many faces". Hopefully Don was not too discouraged when he heard it.

Bob Dylan had been on a never-ending tour since 1988, and 10 years later, Joni joined him on the road. She would have no truck with the loud, "masculine" sound on the stages that the guys loved but which kept bouncing back at her; so she turned hers

RIGHT:
Portrait of Mitchell taken at the Bel Air Hotel November 30, 1996

down and the echoes stopped. Which brought her up against a very unhappy Bob Dylan, because she got a good review and he didn't; the Chicago Tribune had noted "lush tones... Brian Blade dancing with brushes... Mitchell's exquisite guitar voicings". Dylan fired his soundman.

With her quintet including Larry Klein, and her entourage including new boyfriend Don Freed, the potential for friction was ever present; but Don donned his earphones and wisely kept away from any areas that might have produced tension.

The Taming the Tiger album release was the start of almost a decade in which she produced no original new songs. The two albums Both Sides Now, released in the year 2000, and Travelogue, released in 2002, were re-workings of old material; the former contained orchestral arrangements of jazz standards that Joni covered, which garnered good reviews and led to a short national tour, and the latter contained orchestral accompaniments to songs that she had written previously, a far cry from her minimalist days.

The tour covered twelve venues starting in Los Angeles and ending with two concerts at Madison Square Garden, New York. In each city, she played with different orchestras conducted by Vince Mendoza. Backing her were superb musicians; Larry Klein and Herbie Hancock, Wallace Roney on trumpet and Bob Sheppard, saxophone.

It was not surprising, perhaps, that the song that affected everyone most deeply when they heard it, was Joni's reworked version of Both Sides Now; it had been such an iconic song for her, so pivotal to her career. From the pinnacle of a life lived, the song took on new poignancy, of course, it's slow, easy listening style nestling in the lush orchestral arrangement, allowing listeners time to ponder the words she sang; "Leave them laughing when you go and if you can don't let them know, don't give yourself away".

The musicians she played with were in tears, but Joni had not

given herself away and had no need of tears. She did, however, permit herself to feel enormous pleasure at the impact of the song written so many years before by a young woman who had not fully comprehended the depth of the words that she had written, which were given that depth by a woman in her fifties who had lived life to the full.

Joni was not well at the time of the tour, and the weeks on the road were hard on her. It was not an experience she wished to repeat again. Not least because she was unhappy with the quality of the orchestras en route.

Travelogue only managed sales of $72,000 having cost $300,000 to make. Someone had miscalculated. She blamed the record company and was determined once more to quit the business that had "made itself so repugnant to me".

There were, of course, now other people to consider in her life; her daughter and grandchildren, and as she had always maintained that the songwriting began after she had given up her daughter for adoption, finding her again seemed the perfect excuse to quit the business altogether. Motherhood, albeit unfulfilled, had caused her to look at the world through the eyes of a mother and informed her songwriting, she claimed, throughout 30 years when she thought she had been "deeply disturbed emotionally". And when the emotional gloss of the reunion had tarnished, Joni discovered what motherhood can really be like and decided that her daughter was a damaged person.

Kilauren harboured deep resentments towards the mother who had given her away, and the relationship was fostered and festered over the following years. Joni's greatest pleasure, perhaps, from finding her daughter again was in her grandchildren, Marlin and Daisy, who were not burdened with any baggage from the past.

She contented herself with leaving the nuts and bolts of her professional life to others, whilst her seven-year relationship with

RIGHT:
Joni Mitchell at the 43rd Annual Grammy Awards held at the Staples Center, Los Angeles, CA., Feb. 21, 2001

John Freed finally faded into history with the new millennium. Freed went to live in an apartment in Victoria BC, Canada, listening to songs on an old portable record player operated by cranking. Joni must have approved.

Joni went back to her painting and having to cope with the onset of Morgellons syndrome, an unconfirmed skin condition, which causes fibres beneath and embedded in the skin to erupt. The disease caused her to become paranoid, and she damaged her face by pulling at the skin. Mostly she would stay out of the limelight, giving only occasional interviews, dividing her time between the 80 acres of her property in Sechelt, British Columbia, and Los Angeles.

It was only in 2006, that Joni felt the need to get back into the recording studio with a host of new songs in the jazz-pop-rock mould. Her voice was no longer able to leap and dive as it had once, but her vocal cords had benefitted from the long years of rest.

One phone call that pleased Joni at this time, came from Jean Grand-Mâitre, artistic director of the Alberta Ballet. He wanted to use the singer's music in a ballet, an idea which excited Joni immensely.

She did not, however, interfere in any way with the performance, allowing the ballet master the artistic freedom that she would have claimed for herself. The ballet would be called The Fiddle and the Drum, the title of a song that she had first recorded on the 1969 album Clouds; it now became an anti-war song in the era of the Iraq war; "And so once again, oh, America my friend, and so once again, you are fighting us all... we have all come to fear the beating of your drum".

The ballet premiered on February the 8th 2007 in Calgary, Canada, to rapturous applause.

When the album Shine was released in September 2007, the reviewers were falling over themselves with praise, and the track One Week Last Summer, won the Grammy in 2007 for best pop instrumental performance.

Rolling Stone was not convinced; it called her an ageing ecologist "who gives ecology a bad name", mentioning that it was her first album for the Starbucks music label, with whom she had signed a two-year deal, which no doubt caused many to feel that she was having her cake and eating it – and dropping the wrapper on the street, no doubt.

Accompanied by minimal instrumentation – she was playing with musicians she admired; Larry Klein, Brian Blade, Bob Sheppard – her themes were no longer romantic love, there was no room for that in her world that had seen the Iraq war and the ravaging of the environment; "Holy earth how can we heal you? We cover you like blight... if I had a heart I'd cry" she sings on the track If I Had a Heart.

Appropriately, considering her overflowing frustration at the world, the title track, Shine, implores a little light to shine upon all of the injustices and errors and terrors in the world that she lists in her song. And the list of subjects that she wanted that light to shine on could have gone on to infinity; but she chose just a few verses of the many she had written, to represent the others.

Shine rose to number 14 on the Billboard 200 chart, the highest spot in the United States in over 30 years since the release of Hejira.

RIGHT:
Joni's 75th birthday celebration live at The Dorothy Chandler Pavilion on November 7, 2018 in Los Angeles, California

THE CIRCLE CLOSES

Then, apart from two albums of her past work in 2013 and 2014, there was silence.

She wasn't always quiet; in 2010 she accused Bob Dylan of plagiarism only to deny in 2013 that she had made the accusation. It was the same year that she said that she was finally going to quit; she had railed against the world for so long, now she would devote herself to promoting the cause of those diagnosed with Morgellons disease.

Joni made the headlines again in 2015 for a very different reason. On March the 31st, she was found unconscious in the kitchen of her home in Los Angeles. No one found her for three days. Rushed into hospital, she was given emergency surgery, but there was pessimism about the chances of recovery. Fortunately, however, they all proved to be wrong, and although at first, she could not walk, therapy would eventually restore the use of her legs, though it would take several years. Her friend Leslie Morris was appointed her conservator to look after her. After a period in a rehabilitation unit, Joni was allowed to go home and within three months was able to regain some mobility.

Joni celebrated her 75th birthday in 2019, and it seemed as though the entire music world wanted to celebrate with her. There were two tribute concerts to her in Los Angeles in November 2018, when the stars lined up to give their interpretations of her songs with one of the men she admired so greatly, Brian Blade, as co-musical director of the event.

Former lovers turned up; James Taylor, and Graham Nash, who delivered a poignant tribute by singing Our House, the song that he had written when he and Joni were in love and happy domestication in Laurel Canyon.

But many others had come along to fête her, from Rufus Wainwright and Chaka Khan to Emmylou Harris and Kris Kristofferson. Peter Gabriel was there, via Skype at least, to remind everybody that she was "a difficult sod at times" but her music would remain timeless with melodies "like jewels on a trampoline jumping all around".

There was to be another form of celebration to mark the 75th year of Joni Mitchell's roller-coaster life journey. Back in 1971, when her album Blue was rising to the top of the charts, Joni had produced a book of hand-drawn illustrations, poems and lyrics, making just 100 copies

for her friends. She had decided to have it published for the first time on a larger scale. Her publishers echoed the thoughts of many in saying that her influence on popular culture was peerless; there was simply no one else like her.

Joni always considered herself to be outside of the box, which was sometimes a lonely place to be. "I've been excommunicated from every school in music there is" she once said; from folk when she crossed into pop and from jazz and then again when she crossed over into 'hybrid' music. But for her, that was how she kept her music fresh.

"She's probably the best of us" David Crosby pronounced in 2015, "probably the greatest living songwriter."

Joni's musical canvas was a woman searching for answers, and she produced probably the most in-depth chronicle of that search that has ever been created. In the song All I Want, she tells us that "I am on a lonely road and I am travelling looking for the key to set me free".

Whilst remaining the artsy, middle-class painter, she was a genius with words, possessing an unmatched ability to analyse thoughts and sensations about the world that passed before her eyes and pin them up in bright colours for the world to see.

Her view was that "Without emotionality in the arts, it's merely intellectual. It's boring".

As Rolling Stone commented, her songs, like all great art, had been dedicated to illuminating deeper truths, and in the pursuit of those truths she was unafraid to cross boundaries and leave erstwhile disciples and friends behind.

Her insistence on honesty from her heart in her lyrics, and hauntingly beautiful melodies coupled with a voice of unmatched expressive ability, produced music of searing insight that has been an inspiration to many women in the generations of musicians that followed her. Joni Mitchell "is living proof that art endures".

DISCOGRAPHY

STUDIO ALBUMS

SONG TO A SEAGULL	MARCH 1968	189 (US)		
CLOUDS	MAY 1969	22 (CAN)	31 (US)	
LADIES OF THE CANYON	APRIL 1970	24 (UK)	105 (US)	
BLUE	JUNE 1971	9 (CAN)	15 (US)	3 (UK)
FOR THE ROSES	NOVEMBER 1972	5 (CAN)	11 (US)	
COURT AND SPARK	JANUARY 1974	1 (CAN)	2 (US)	14 (UK)
THE HISSING OF SUMMER LAWNS	NOVEMBER 1975	7 (CAN)	4 (US)	14 (UK)
HEJIRA	NOVEMBER 1976	22 (CAN)	13 (US)	11 (UK)
DON JUAN'S RECKLESS.DAUGHTER	DECEMBER 1977	28 (CAN)	25 (US)	20 (UK)
MINGUS	JUNE 1979	37 (CAN)	17 (US)	24 (UK)
WILD THINGS RUN FAST	OCTOBER 1982	33 (CAN)	25 (US)	32 (UK)
DOG EAT DOG	OCTOBER 1985	44 (CAN)	63 (US)	57 (UK)
CHALK MARK IN A RAINSTORM	23RD MARCH 1988	3 (CAN)	45 (US)	26 (UK)
NIGHT RIDE HOME	19TH FEBRUARY 1991	29 (CAN)	41 (US)	25 (UK)
TURBULENCE INDIGO	25TH OCTOBER 1994	24 (CAN)	47 (US)	53 (UK)
TAMING THE TIGER	29TH SEPTEMBER 1998	86 (CAN)	75 (US)	57 (UK)
BOTH SIDES NOW	20TH MARCH 2000	19 (CAN)	66 (US)	50 (UK)
TRAVELOGUE	19TH NOVEMBER 2002			
SHINE	25TH SEPTEMBER 2007	13 (CAN)	14 (US)	36 (UK)

LIVE ALBUMS

MILES OF AISLES	NOVEMBER 1974	13 (CAN)	2 (US)	34 (UK)
SHADOWS AND LIGHT	SEPTEMBER 1980	73 (CAN)	38 (US)	63 (UK)

COMPILATION ALBUMS

HITS	29TH OF OCTOBER 1996	161 (US)	
MISSES	29TH OF OCTOBER 1996		
THE COMPLETE GEFFEN RECORDINGS	23RD OF SEPTEMBER 2003		
THE BEGINNING OF SURVIVAL	27TH OF JULY 2004		
DREAMLAND	14TH OF SEPTEMBER 2004	177 (US)	43 (UK)
STARBUCKS' ARTISTS CHOICE	2005		
SONG OF A PRAIRIE GIRL	26TH OF APRIL 2005		
STUDIO ALBUMS 1968 – 1979	12TH OF FEBRUARY 2013		
LOVE HAS MANY FACES, A QUARTET, A BALLET, WAITING TO BE DANCED	24TH OF NOVEMBER 2014		

GUEST SINGLES

JANET JACKSON GOT 'TIL IT'S GONE	1997	19 (CAN	6 (US)	6 (UK)

SINGLES

NIGHT IN THE CITY	1968		
CHELSEA MORNING	1969		
BIG YELLOW TAXI	1970	14 (CAN)	11 (UK)
CAREY	1971	27 (CAN)	93 (US
CALIFORNIA	1971		
YOU TURN ME ON, I'M A RADIO	1972	10 (CAN)	
COLD BLUE STEEL AND SWEET FIRE	1973		
RAISED ON ROBBERY	1973	51 (CAN)	
HELP ME	1974	6 (CAN)	
FREE MAN IN PARIS	1974	16 (CAN)	
BIG YELLOW TAXI (LIVE)	1974	54 (CAN)	
CAREY (LIVE)	1974		
IN FRANCE THEY KISS ON MAIN STREET	1976	19 (CAN)	
COYOTE	1977	79 (CAN)	
OFF NIGHT BACKSTREET	1978		
JERICHO	1978		
THE DRY CLEANER FROM DES MOINES	1979		

WHY DO FOOLS FALL IN LOVE	1980		
(YOU'RE SO SQUARE) BABY I DON'T CARE	1982		
CHINESE CAFE	1983		
GOOD FRIENDS	1985		
SHINY TOYS	1986		
LIFE ON MARS	1973		
MY SECRET PLACE	1988	44 (CAN)	
SNAKES AND LADDERS	1988		
COOL WATER	1988		
NIGHT RIDE HOME	1991		
COME IN FROM THE COLD	1991	27 (CAN)	
HOW DO YOU STOP	1994	56 (CAN)	100 (UK)
SEX KILLS	1994	68 (CAN)	
SUNNY SUNDAY	1994		
THE CRAZY CRIES OF LOVE	1998		
BOTH SIDES, NOW	2000